BABIES

How to Afford Your Bundle of Joy

A CPA Canada Book

LISA VAN DE GEYN
with Vivian Leung, CPA, CA

Cormorant Books

The publisher gratefully acknowledges the support of the Canada Council for the Arts and the Ontario Arts Council for its publishing program. We acknowledge the financial support of the Government of Canada through the Canada Book Fund (CBF) for our publishing activities, and the Government of Ontario through Ontario Creates, an agency of the Ontario Ministry of Culture, and the Ontario Book Publishing Tax Credit Program.

LIBRARY AND ARCHIVES CANADA CATALOGUING IN PUBLICATION

Title: Babies: how to afford your bundle of joy /
Lisa van de Geyn with Vivian Leung, CPA, CA.
Other titles: Babie$
Names: Van de Geyn, Lisa, author. | Leung, Vivian, 1976– author.
Description: Series statement: A CPA Canada book |
Revision of: Babie$: the real cost of babies / Lisa van de Geyn.
Identifiers: Canadiana (print) 20200268945 | Canadiana (ebook) 20200268953 |
ISBN 9781770866096 (softcover) | ISBN 9781770866102 (EPUB)
Subjects: LCSH: Parents—Finance, Personal. | LCSH: Child rearing—Economic aspects. |
LCSH: Families—Economic aspects.
Classification: LCC HG179 .V35 2020 | DCC 332.0240085—dc23

Cover design: Angel Guerra / Archetype
Interior text design: Tannice Goddard / tannicegdesigns.ca
Printer: Friesens

Printed and bound in Canada.

CORMORANT BOOKS INC.
260 SPADINA AVENUE, SUITE 502, TORONTO, ON, M5T 2E4
www.cormorantbooks.com

For Ad, Peyps, Sebastian and Nicky —
the four kids I spend too much money on.
— Lisa van de Geyn

To Brandon and Callie —
you two have been worth every penny.
— Vivian Leung

Contents

CHAPTER ONE

So You're Going to Have a Baby!

YOU'VE TAKEN THE pregnancy tests, made the big announcement, and you've probably caught a glimpse of your baby on a sonogram. You're taking prenatal vitamins, designing the nursery, and mulling over potential girls' and boys' names. If you're like the majority of Canadians, there are probably a few things you haven't added to your pre-baby to-do list:

- put together a baby budget
- figure out your expenses
- think about what parental leave will mean to your bank account

This is an exciting time — you'll soon be holding your bundle of joy! But get ready: he or she will also require a bundle of cash.

How Much Does It Cost to Raise a Child Today?

That's a tough one. In September 2013, the Fraser Institute set out to answer this convoluted question in their report *The Cost of Raising Children*, authored by Christopher A. Sarlo. Before the author's analysis of expenses and scenarios, he came to one important conclusion: it would be virtually impossible to determine the cost of a child using one simple formula. In fact, he wasn't able to arrive at an "official cost of children or methodology to determine this very important calculation."

The report went on to look at other published estimates over the years.

- In 2011, in an issue of *MoneySense* magazine, an article entitled "The real cost of raising kids" gave a well-researched dollar amount for raising a child from birth to age nineteen: $12,825 per year, for a total of about $243,660.
- In 2015, Statistics Canada found, according to average household expenditures, that the total spending of couples with children versus couples without children was $117,386 and $82,945 respectively, suggesting families with kids spent $34,441 more than their childless counterparts. This figure didn't answer "how much do kids cost?" but simply showed the difference in expenditures between these two groups, and it may not have addressed the variables, including the spending changes which arise when a baby arrives (e.g., their research showed that parents tend to spend less on going to restaurants and more at the grocery store when a child is born).

The Fraser Institute's report reached a figure much less daunting than others that have been published: only $3,000 to $4,000 a year. It's important to note that the author came to this conclusion by excluding child care from the findings and basing the annual expenditure on parents being very careful with their money (e.g., growing their own vegetables, using coupons religiously, and looking for hand-me-downs).

While there doesn't seem to be one specific amount of money experts will agree on, there are no two ways about it — raising kids definitely costs a pretty penny. The good news is that while having a baby will be an expensive endeavour, there are trade-offs you can make to your lifestyle to make having a baby — and the price tag attached to it — more manageable.

I have a confession to make: I didn't know what I was getting into financially when I had my first daughter back in 2008. Like most parents-to-be, my husband and I got wrapped up in the sheer excitement of the pregnancy — and all the shopping for baby gear! We knew our bank account would take a hit when I went on maternity leave, but we were, well, oblivious to just how difficult it would be to make ends meet. I didn't know nearly enough about how maternity leave and employment insurance worked. We didn't prepare — we didn't budget, we didn't try living off less money, we didn't work to pay off credit cards. The problem was that we didn't really change anything, and that was foolish.

Which brings me to my second confession: We obviously didn't learn from our first pregnancy, because two years and three days later, when we were in the same position and our second daughter was born, we weren't even remotely financially ready. In fact, things got even harder. We had already experienced a year of maternity leave and employment insurance, and we were about to enter into the same scenario — another year without one full-time salary. Not only did we not try to modify our spending habits and behaviour when I was pregnant, we didn't change anything when we were one income down. It's not like we have a lavish lifestyle, but we should've been careful and, dare I say, stingy — we should've cut down on our spending the first time, especially knowing we were hoping to have two kids fairly close together. But you know what they say — hindsight is 20/20. If I'd known then what I know now, I would've found a budget template and sought the help of a financial expert to get us on the right track.

In the chapters that follow, you'll find plenty of ways you can save a few dollars. To give you the most bang for your buck, and to ensure you get the most up-to-date, knowledgeable advice out there, I turned to a handful of financial experts for help. The chartered professional accountants you'll meet are well versed in everything from the benefits of setting up Registered Education Savings Plans (RESPs) and what maternity and parental leave will mean when it's tax time to the payments you're entitled to from the government after you deliver your baby and advice on getting by on employment insurance.

But first, let's talk about why it's so important to budget for a baby.

Why Should You Budget?

Whether you spend as little as $4,500 or as much as the estimated $12,825 per year, getting your finances ready before your baby is born should be as important to you as your regular checkups with your doctor or midwife. The Financial Consumer Agency of Canada warns parents-to-be to prepare for sticker shock by coming up with a budget before your baby is born: "The better shape your finances are in, the more options you will have when it comes to maternity and parental leave," the website explains.

"Usually one or both parents will take some time off work once the baby is born, so it's good to get financial matters sorted out well beforehand. As soon as you and your partner decide to have a baby, or as soon as you find out you're expecting, it's best to determine how you can live off one person's income and put that into practice before the baby arrives," suggests Cynthia Kett, CPA, CA, CGA. She makes a good point!

You'll find there's a steep learning curve when welcoming a baby, and many soon-to-be parents haven't thought through the potential change to their financial situation, in part because of the unknown.

Kett outlines a few things for you to consider before getting pregnant or, at the latest, bringing home a baby. These and other topics are discussed in the chapters listed below. You'll also find plenty of tips from parents who, like you, weren't 100 percent sure what a new addition to the family would look like — emotionally, physically, socially, and especially financially!

Things You Should Consider

Have You Researched the Cost of Everything Your Baby Will Need?

We're talking diapers to formula, cribs to strollers, breast pumps to baby food jars (which, by the way, have gone up an average of fifteen cents per jar in the past few years). Parents-to-be are usually so excited to shop for baby things that they don't pay attention to the high cost of items, and many stock up on things they likely won't ever use. A baby carriage, for example, didn't cost much more than about $30 in the early 1980s. Today, you could easily spend a few thousand on a "travel system" (a deluxe stroller and car seat combo). While it's possible to spend thousands of dollars on baby accoutrements, you don't need to, and you shouldn't go into debt to outfit your child.

Chapter 2 looks at the costs associated with bringing home your little one, as well as how to be frugal when shopping for baby gear.

Will You Be Able to Stay Off Work and Take Maternity Leave? Will Your Partner Take Parental Leave?

For most Canadians, the basic rate for calculating your employment insurance (EI) benefits is 55 percent of your average insurable weekly earnings (up to a maximum amount). In 2020, the maximum yearly insurable earnings amount is $54,200, which means you can receive a maximum of $573 per week (assuming you take the standard one-year leave). You can also opt to take a leave of eighteen months; your EI benefits will be spread over the course of your leave. (Note: EI benefits are considered taxable, so the actual amount you take home will be less than this.)

Chapter 3 looks at maternity and parental leave, as well as EI and what to expect when it comes to your income taxes.

How Much Will Child Care Cost?

In a perfect world, you'll have family who live around the corner who will insist on helping you with child care. Full disclosure — this is the lucky situation we found ourselves in. My mother has been a stay-at-home parent since I was born, and she was only too happy to take my daughters when I went back to work, saving us tens of thousands of dollars in child care. But if you're not that lucky, whichever child care option you end up choosing will definitely increase your costs. Depending on where you live, the price of daycare is the same as the cost for one year of university. (In fact, in big cities, it can cost even more!) "We didn't have family living nearby as both sets of grandparents were in Quebec at the time and we lived in Ontario," says Virginia Tang, CPA,

CA. "We found a hybrid approach to daycare can help reduce costs. For example, we used a friend (home-based daycare) two days a week and shared a spot at a local daycare the other three days. This was the arrangement with our first child. After we had our second, we decided to employ a live-in nanny, but also continued to send both children to daycare on a part-time basis."

When it comes down to it, researching your options will make you feel much more comfortable about your decision. That's how Debra King, CPA, CMA, says she felt before her baby was born. "After adjusting to the idea that I was going to be a parent, I sat down and made a list of everything to do with having a baby. One was child care. I made a list of all my possible options — I could stay home, my husband could stay home, family, friends, daycare, nanny, home daycare," she says. After going through each option to see what was feasible and how each would affect her finances, she was down to three possibilities that each cost money. "The most expensive were hiring a nanny and daycare. Child care took a huge chunk out of our monthly budget, especially when we had two children. At times I wondered if one of us should stay at home. It all comes down to what's best for you, your child, and your finances," she says.

If you go the daycare centre route, be prepared, as centres in some cities have long waiting lists. If you prefer in-home care, finding a nanny isn't always easy. Neither option is inexpensive. After determining what child care costs will be, some couples realize their best bet is to arrange their work and finances so that one or both parents can care for their children at home.

Beyond financial considerations, you'll want to decide whether you want to go back to work following your leave. You'll likely have no idea how you will feel about leaving the baby until after he or she is born, so it may be difficult to figure out whether you'll want to head back to your day job. Your mind may change once you've experienced what it's like to be home with your little one and — if you have a partner who continues to work post-baby — after you've spent some time living on one salary. "The decision to work or stay at home is really very personal, and it's influenced by the parents' philosophy toward child-rearing as

well as their financial situation," Tang says. "Some believe it's more beneficial for the child if one parent is home during the early years, while
others think the opposite. Personally, I believe if you can afford high-
quality daycare, have a supportive work environment, and enjoy your
job, I would say it's a good idea to continue working, as the cost of
raising a child only increases with age."

Read about the cost of child care and going back to work in Chapter 4.

What Other Assistance Are You Entitled to from the Federal and Provincial Governments Once You Become a Parent?

Find out about the benefits you can receive in Chapter 5.

Do You Have the Money to Open a Registered Education Savings Plan (RESP)?

"Parents should take full advantage of an RESP; with post-secondary
costs escalating, every bit helps," says Kett. "The sooner you start an
RESP, the more time the contributions have to increase in value." That's
true, but there's an incredible amount of information to learn in order to
really benefit from RESPs. Plus, not everyone will be in the position to
open this savings vehicle for their child. Should you pay off your credit
card debt before starting an RESP? You'll read about this and much
more in Chapter 6. You'll also find out how the government can assist in
saving for your child's education.

Will You Be Able to Afford It If and When You're Ready to Have Another Baby?

Adding to your family might end up meaning moving to a larger home
and buying a family-sized car(s). You might love your one-bedroom
condo in the city if you live alone or with your partner, but you'll find it
will get crowded quickly with the arrival of a baby or two.

"If you're planning on having another child, you already know how
much it costs. Yes, you will have some hand-me-downs from your first,
but can your life fit another person? How will your life change with
another person in it? Do you have room? Will your car fit another baby
seat? These seem like mundane questions, but they're often forgotten

questions," says King. "I had a four-door sedan. You'd think that it would be fine for four people, but I found that just because you have four doors doesn't mean it easily carries all the stuff you need for two babies and a dog. I dreaded grocery shopping with two babies. Where was I going to put everything? In the end I had to trade my car in for a van," she says, adding that the swap didn't help her finances because she hadn't planned for it. The take-away? Don't wait until your second (or third) baby arrives to plan — do it now! You'll have more options and time if you start putting things in place well before your due date.

Get more details on adding to your household in Chapter 7.

Still Have Questions?

It's true — there's a lot to know, understand, and prep for when you're expecting a little one! If you want more information on a certain subject that's mentioned in one or more of the seven chapters here, not to worry. In Chapter 8 you'll find some of the best resources that were used in putting this book together. (The homework is done for you!)

CHAPTER TWO

Budgeting for Baby

AFTER TWO WEEKS of nursing, first-time mom Jennifer made the decision to switch her newborn daughter, Paige, from breastfeeding to formula. That night, her husband, John, ran out to their North Toronto neighbourhood's twenty-four-hour supermarket to pick up a case of formula that her pediatrician had recommended. When John got home with a case of formula and a receipt in hand, he looked at Jennifer and grinned. "Do you have any idea how expensive this stuff is? It was $53, so I'm guessing it will last a couple of weeks, right?"

How much did opting for formula end up costing Jennifer and John?

For the sake of convenience, John picked up a case of the ready-to-feed variety (instead of the less expensive powder or concentrate). There are eighteen eight-ounce cans in each case. Cans are only usable for twenty-four hours after opening (if refrigerated) and for one hour after pouring into a bottle. They figured Paige would need to eat about three ounces at a time, so they'd get almost three feedings from each can.

Newborns eat every three or four hours around the clock, so Paige would need to eat about eight times a day. At three ounces per feeding, she'd go through almost three bottles per can. Over twenty-four hours, she'd eat about three cans worth of formula, which added up to approximately twenty-one cans per week. So a case would last for only about six days, meaning the couple would need to buy five or six cases a month!

What they didn't take into consideration (understandably, as new parents) was that there would be many a feed when Paige would want either a little more than three ounces or only an ounce or two. There would even be times when Jennifer or John would make a bottle then take Paige out of her crib and try to feed her, but with no success. An hour and a half later, she'd wake up hungry, and the bottle they'd made earlier would have to be thrown away and a new bottle made. They figured about 5 percent of the formula they bought was wasted and ended up down the drain.

During the newborn stage, John and Jennifer spent about $270 to $320 (plus tax) per month on formula. Little did they know it would be a much different, more costly story a couple of months later when Paige would start eating twice that amount!

Do Your Research

Few activities are more exciting for a soon-to-be or new parent than spending hours Googling everything from prenatal nutrition to newborn development, from Braxton Hicks to the pros and cons of Pitocin — it's certainly more interesting than researching "saving for baby" or information on RESPs. But there's a major category that expectant parents can get really wrapped up in: baby gear.

New parents generally have a kilometre-long list of wants and needs for their bundle of joy, but it doesn't come cheap. "Babies are expensive — it's hard to imagine that these little people can cost so much, but baby and toddler furniture, clothing, and diapers can really add up," says Kett. "Baby things are so cute, and the event is so exciting, that it's easy to get carried away."

She's right — according to parenting magazines and online parenting sites, some families spend $10,000 or more on their baby's first twelve months, and that's not taking child care into account (i.e., if you can't or don't want to stay home for your entire maternity or parental leave). Check out Babies R Us, for example — there are more than fifty categories of items for the newborn to one-year age group, from bibs and burp cloths to strollers and diaper bags, play yards and bassinets to change tables and diaper pails, pacifiers and exersaucers to high chairs and bouncers, and within each category, parents-to-be will have myriad brands, colours, sizes, etc., to choose from. It's an endless list!

Here's the thing: It's easy to get caught up in the hype of wanting to make sure your baby has the best. "I remember buying stuff for my daughter. I wanted so badly to have the best because nothing was too good for her. But then reality set in. We couldn't afford it," says King. "After I got over feeling stressed and upset that my baby wasn't going to get the best, I asked myself, 'Will this make my baby any less happy if she doesn't have this?' The answer was no."

Han Shu, CPA, CA, agrees and adds that folks need to consider functionality as well as price points. "I've seen people who don't make big bucks buy top-of-the-line items, and that really caused them damage financially. Most baby products on the market have been screened for safety, so they're really not different function-wise. It's just some specific features and brand names that set them apart."

Tang offers this advice. "The decision about what type and brand of baby gear you're considering is really the basic issue of needs and wants. Your child will certainly not know whether he or she is sitting in a $1,000-plus stroller versus one that's much less. Think about borrowing gear or buying used items," she says. "Parents should realize that the infant stage passes very quickly and keeping up with the Joneses is not financially responsible and not attainable." So, suggests Tang, if you're a parent who focuses more on preparing financially for the future costs of raising children, the "needs versus wants" decision is an easy one.

The truth is, it's tough to figure out what you'll need when you're a first-time, sleep-deprived, time-pressed parent, so researching your options before making decisions will end up saving you money in the long run. Ask your friends with kids their opinions on cloth versus disposable diapers and strollers versus travel systems, as well as what you need to buy before or as soon as the baby is born and what you can wait to get a few months down the road. And don't forget — babies grow like weeds, so spending a ton on clothing is often a waste. This is the kind of research that will be invaluable to you.

FINANCIAL TIPS

Budgeting was crucial to our family financial planning when we were pregnant with our first child, Noah. It was critical for us to understand our cash flows, current spending habits, and future child care costs so that we could be adaptable and prepared. But this is a tall order all at once. So the first thing we did in month three of our pregnancy was track our expenses and spending habits for two weeks. Today, there are all sorts of apps to help you do this simply and as easily as possible. We then researched all of the future costs that we could have in the first twelve months of our son's life. We included diapers, formula, and clothes. But this can be variable for each new parent, depending on your choices (such as disposable diapers versus cloth diapers). But after month five, we had a budget for our monthly expenditures for our first twelve months with Noah, based on tracking our spending and estimating the baby costs. This was important to see if we needed to curtail certain discretionary spending (such as eating out or saving more for future financial goals such as a registered education savings plan). My key message: Track your expenses and add for your expected costs of your child as soon as you can.

— Garth Sheriff, CPA, CA, dad of two

Expenses You'll Encounter

Nursery Furniture

Outfitting your baby's bedroom is a fun thing to do, even for those who despise decorating. If you're going for the basics, you can keep it simple:

- a crib (depending on where you go, priced from about $50 to $2,500+)
- a mattress (from $100 to $200+)
- a change table ($200 to $400+) plus a change pad (about $20+)
- a cozy rocker for feeding ($300 to $400+)

However, there are so many more options, e.g., blankets and bedding, storage, rugs, lighting, mobiles, pictures, custom drapes, and room-darkening blinds. With seemingly countless choices available, it's hard to keep it simple!

Feeding

If you decide to breastfeed, formula feed, or combine the two, you might want to buy:

- a nursing pillow ($30 to $60)
- nursing covers ($15 to $40+)
- a breast pump (from about $60 for a manual pump to $350+ for an electric one)
- a few bottles

Depending on the type of formula you decide to use, your choices are:

- about $25 for a 900mL container of powder to $50+ for a case of eighteen cans of the ready-to-feed variety
- plenty of bottles (from about $5 to $15+ per bottle) — don't be surprised if you have to try a few different brands and types of bottles and nipples to find out what your baby prefers
- a bottle warmer (about $50+) for making a batch of bottles each day then refrigerating them and heating them as needed; these are also helpful if you continue to nurse and pump when you go back to work
- a steam sterilizer (from $30 to $100+) if you aren't into boiling pots full of bottles to sterilize!

Once your baby has reached the cereal, fruit, and veggie stage, you can expect these expenses:

- cereal (about $5 per box)
- baby food (about $1 per jar)

- a high chair (once your baby can sit up on his or her own, $85 to $400+)

Travel

This is where the costs get higher, but your baby's safety is most important, so this is not the best time to penny-pinch.

You will need a car seat, a car seat base, and a reliable stroller.

- an infant car seat/carrier ($200 to $400+) is well worth the expense as your baby's safety in the car is so important (also, many hospitals will not let you leave with your baby if you don't have an infant car seat). You can also get adapters for most models that allow you to click the seat into your stroller (this means you don't have to fiddle with putting your stroller together in a busy parking lot — you can take the bucket seat out and snap it on to the chassis and go). Many work well for babies from four pounds to about thirty pounds (but this option means you'll need to purchase an infant/child seat within the year).
- or you can opt for an infant/child car seat ($150 to $450+), which will convert from a rear-facing infant seat (suitable for babies from five to forty-five pounds) to a forward-facing toddler seat (for twenty-two to sixty-five pounds)
- a car seat base ($25 to $100) is necessary for using the seat in your car
- a full-sized single stroller ($250 to $3,000)

Or you can buy all these components in an all-in-one travel system, which is costlier but a good value because the stroller can be used after your child outgrows the infant car seat ($650 to $3,000).

Safety for your baby is paramount, and this equipment is your biggest financial commitment, so you should research your options thoroughly. Talk to other parents and Google each component or the travel systems. One helpful site is www.canadianfamily.ca/baby-gear-guide.

Infant Care

From diapers and baby monitors to safety gates and teething rings, there's no shortage of items you can put on your list. Some examples are:

- diaper pails (about $35, plus $10 for a roll of bags)
- health care kits (with thermometer and aspirator, among other items, $20)
- humidifiers (up to $80)
- diaper rash cream ($10)
- diaper wipes ($5 for one tub)
- a newborn-to-toddler bathtub ($20 to $40)
- shampoo-sized bottles of gentle head-to-toe soap (about $6)

Also, don't forget teething toys (the iconic teething toy Sophie the Giraffe is about $30).

The biggest expense in this category? Diapers. You will find the cloth versus disposable diaper debate is often a contentious one, so choose the option that works best for your family (and your wallet!). If you decide to use cloth, there are plenty of choices so prices will vary. They will cost you about $20 per diaper (or nearly $500 for a pile of twenty-four diapers!), which you will have to wash and dry on your own (you'll want plenty on hand so you're not washing diapers night and day). If you hire a diaper service — they deliver clean diapers and pick up soiled ones — this convenience can cost $25+ per week, depending on where you live.

PARENT'S TIP

My husband and I have been surprised by how much friends and family have helped us out financially. Whether it's food, baby gear, maternity hand-me-downs, new clothes, big-ticket items from grandparents (a stroller and rocker), or Registered Education Savings Plan contributions, everyone wants to help out, and the generosity has been overwhelming. You really don't have to, and shouldn't, buy all the baby stuff yourself.

— Amy, mom of one

The disposable variety of diaper is comparable in cost to using a cloth diaper service — a box of eighty-eight newborn diapers costs about $35. At first, you'll be changing diapers at least eight times a day, which means a box will last you about eleven days. So, it will cost you about $100 per month for diapers. (Diaper changes will become less frequent eventually, but newborn babies don't do much more than eat, sleep, and poop!)

Clothing and Accessories

Buying lots of onesies, sleepers, layette sets, bibs, hats, socks, no-scratch mittens, and adorable little outfits is hard to resist. You'll want to stock up on onesies, sleepers, and bibs because (between the spit-up and diaper explosions) babies can go through many wardrobe changes each day. Baby wear doesn't have to be expensive (as long as you're not planning on dressing your little one in designer labels), but it won't be cheap to fill his or her closet with cute outfits.

Toys

Parents rave about their bouncers, exersaucers, and swings — not only do they provide entertainment and distraction for your baby, but they are lifesavers for parents. (You'll appreciate being able to put your baby down to make a sandwich or run to the bathroom once in a while without having to carry your little one with you.) You might opt for:

- a bouncer ($40 to $300)
- an exersaucer ($25 to $200)
- a swing ($75 to $300)
- or all three!

Other options include:

- activity play mats (about $50 to $150) to keep babies entertained when they're on their backs, plus they're perfect for tummy time
- clip toys (used on strollers and car seats) are popular, as are soft plush and squeeze toys, blocks, rattles, and other fun items

Toys for tots can cost from $4 for a small toy to about $150 for a deluxe play mat decked out with lights, sound, and music.

How to Be Frugal

It's certainly possible to get the equipment you want and the supplies you need without spending a fortune. Here are some ideas for how to keep this event as inexpensive as possible.

Have a Baby Shower

If your best friend, sister, colleague, neighbour, or anyone else has offered to fête you and your soon-to-be addition, thank them and graciously accept. Julie Blais Comeau, chief etiquette officer at etiquettejulie.com, says people understand that the main reason for having a party is to shower the expectant mother with things she needs for her new arrival. "The exclusive purpose of these parties is to offer gifts; as adults, we all know what showers mean." Go ahead and fill up your registry at your favourite baby store — friends and family will often pitch in for a bigger item, and the parents in attendance will have a good idea of what you need, especially if you're a first-timer.

Buy Second-Hand

If you're pregnant or have just welcomed your first child, here's a piece of advice you'll be glad to have down the road: Kids grow out of their clothes so fast that you'll end up with drawers full of outfits that were either worn once or twice or have never seen the light of day. The last time I added up the price tags still attached to clothes that my kids never wore, the amount was more than $200! If friends or family offer you hand-me-downs, don't turn down their generosity.

This second-hand rule should also be applied to maternity clothes. If someone's willing to lend or give you pieces, you'll save a lot. My best friend and sister happily wore the pile of freshly laundered shirts, pants, and dresses I packed up for them. Besides hand-me-downs, keep your eyes open for great deals on "previously loved" clothing and baby gear at yard sales, swap meets, and consignment shops. Join a local parent-to-parent group on Facebook, where you're sure to find a gold mine of low-cost bits and pieces. And search Kijiji, Craigslist, and eBay for great finds.

A final note on buying used baby gear (such as car seats, cribs, and swings) — be sure to do some investigating to make sure the product complies with Health Canada's current safety standards before making deals. Car seats, for example, have expiry dates that you'll need to check; plus, you should never purchase a seat that has been involved in a car accident, so ask the seller for the item's history.

Go Online

Manufacturers of baby products love sending free samples of products and coupons to both expectant and new parents. Many companies offer perks for signing up on their sites and will lavish you with gifts (some send diaper bags, others send formula samples, for example) for doing so.

Many online retailers now offer delivery of baby items right to your door. If you're placing orders every month, some take 5 percent off. If you order from online retailers, be sure to sign up for an online saving service like Ebates.ca, which allows you to shop at these retailers (and a host of others) and get money back on every order you place.

While you're searching for deals, it's a good idea to start building up your supplies when you find sales — think diaper wipes, formula (check the expiry date), baby cereal, jars of food, baby shampoo, detergent for baby's clothes, etc. You'll want to keep an eye out for discounts on diapers, but don't stockpile — babies grow out of diapers very quickly. You might also end up discovering that your child does better in one brand over another (e.g., doesn't leak), so it's best not to hoard. If you do end up with diapers you're not using, you can usually return unopened boxes, or consider donating them to women's shelters.

> ### PARENT'S TIP
>
> When we had Clark, we did different things to save money. I started looking for coupons for groceries and I price matched to get the best deals. I also started taking advantage of stores that have specials and give away gift cards when you purchase something, like Shoppers Drug Mart.
>
> — Hilary, mom of two

> ### HOW THEY DO IT
>
> Kate, seven months pregnant with her first child, went to her sister for advice on what to buy and how much to spend on her upcoming arrival before she and her partner, Cheryl, started shopping for baby gear. "My sister is usually pretty frugal, but even she overspent when she had my nephew. She admits to getting a bit caught up in the excitement and went overboard on a few items. That's definitely something we want to avoid, so I started scouring social media. I joined a bunch of local buy-and-sell Facebook groups and found amazing deals, like gently used clothes, diapers, a baby bathtub, monitors, and a bouncer. We've easily saved hundreds of dollars going this route."

The Hidden Costs

Surprise! Most parents are so busy getting the must-haves and nice-to-haves on their list that they don't consider the less glamorous optional costs that can add up.

Doulas

Whether you've decided on a hospital or home birth with an obstetrician or a midwife delivering your new arrival, doulas act as an extra emotional and physical support person for a specified number of visits before birth, during labour, and after you welcome your baby. (You might consider hiring a doula, especially if you don't have family or friends nearby who can assist you during or after the birth.) The total price for a doula's services can range from about $300 to $1,500, but the typical price in many urban areas ranges from $500 to $900.

Prenatal Classes

They're not mandatory, but it's better to have some informed knowledge of the birthing process and your options during it. Consider taking a class when you're twenty-eight to thirty-seven weeks pregnant and not only will you learn the basics of labour and delivery (complete with a tour of a hospital's prenatal and postpartum wings), but you'll also get plenty of practice in diapering and learning how to nurse (with dolls, of course). Your partner is also bound to get a healthy dose of delivery room etiquette, including plenty of dos (helping your significant other to focus, staying awake while she's dealing with brutal contractions) and don'ts (continuously staring at your phone or watching whatever golf championship is playing on the TV screen in the room).

PARENT'S TIP
"Ask your OB/GYN if the hospital they are affiliated with offers a course, because many hospital programs are more cost-efficient than private programs."   — Jill, mom of two

Family-Friendly Vehicles

Still driving around town in your tiny (but cherished) Smart car? A sporty coupe won't cut it when you go from a household of two to a household of three (or more). It's something you might not have considered when you bought your last car, but you'll need something bigger (at least something with a back seat) with a baby on the way, and certainly if you're thinking about having a couple of kids. Four doors are also much better when you are manoeuvring a baby in a car seat into the back seat! Minivans and sport-utility vehicles are even better for a family, but they don't come cheap — you could spend anywhere from about $20,000 to more than $100,000.

PARENT'S TIP
"Before kids, a minivan might seem like a bad dream. But once you're a family of four and have kids in soccer, plus carpooling duty, your outlook changes."   — Dan, dad of two

Cord Blood Banking

You will probably get details on banking your baby's cord blood when you take prenatal classes. You can have the leftover blood in your baby's umbilical cord collected after birth and kept in a private or public blood bank. This blood contains stem cells, which have the potential to grow into bone marrow cells, brain cells, or other cells to help treat sickle cell disease, leukemia, thalassemia, and Hodgkin's lymphoma. At the present time, doctors generally believe there is only a slight chance that a child will ever use his or her own cord blood, so that's not the best reason to save it. However, if you already have another child who is ill, he or she could greatly benefit. You could donate the blood to a public blood bank, where it would likely be used for treatments for other children who need stem cells for survival. You also have the choice of donating the cord blood for research to help make improvements in these types of treatments in the future. Private banking is typically reserved for siblings, and it's expensive — there's an initial fee of about $1,500 to $2,000, then a storage fee of about $200 per year for as long as the blood is stored. Your best bet is to discuss your options with your health care provider and get more information about the pros and cons of banking your cord blood.

The Costs of Getting Pregnant

Most of us assume we will be able to get pregnant and give birth to our own child. However, there are an increasing number of couples who turn to fertility treatments and adoption in order to realize their dream of having a family. The following are examples of some of the costs involved in these options.

Fertility Treatments

Though doctors agree that infertility is a disease of the reproductive organs, some fertility treatments used to help couples who can't otherwise conceive a child aren't covered by government health insurance and are paid for by the prospective parents.

Folks who live in Quebec are at an advantage: the provincial government covers all treatments, including in vitro fertilization (IVF). Residents in Manitoba receive assistance via a tax credit for paying for their treatments, and, as of 2016, those in Ontario who qualify can receive artificial insemination, one IVF cycle, and one fertility preservation cycle. (Note: Waitlists can be especially long in Ontario. It can take up to several years for a funded cycle.)

While prices of procedures vary depending on where you live, you can expect to pay:

- about $7,000 to $15,000+ per IVF cycle (including drugs)
- about $1,500+ for a frozen embryo transfer
- about $500+ for a cycle of sperm wash and intrauterine insemination (IUI)
- about $1,500+ for an intracytoplasmic sperm injection (ICSI)

Note: Some or all of these treatments may be covered by your employee group health benefits, so check with your insurer. Also, any out-of-pocket costs can be claimed as medical costs on your tax return, so keep all of your documentation and receipts.

HOW THEY DO IT

"We talked a lot about finances prior to getting pregnant because we went through fertility treatments, so we knew that multiples could be a possibility. And with that, we'd be looking at double — or triple — the cost of everything," says Liz, a thirty-something in Vancouver.

Now the parents of twenty-month-old twins, Liz and Chris decided Liz would take eighteen months of leave from her job. "Financially, it was only possible with my husband working two full-time jobs, and with a few changes we made while I was pregnant," she says. "Before maternity leave, I bought a year's worth of wipes and diapers in various sizes so that we wouldn't need to worry about buying them later. I also signed up for an app that offers grocery deals, and we started price matching."

HOW THEY DO IT Cont.
While Liz and Chris were prepared for some of the costs incurred when a new baby is born, there were surprises they weren't anticipating. "Our babies were in the neonatal intensive care unit for eighty-one days, and we ended up spending $1,000 in hospital parking fees," she says.
"Daycare was another thing we didn't quite figure out prior to the kids being born. Child care is expensive for one kid, but with twins, we didn't know what we'd do. I work one or two days a week, and my father offered to watch the girls when I'm not home. Daycare would've been about $3,000 per month, and we couldn't justify paying that amount."

Adoption

Adoptive parents will need to buy all the same equipment as biological parents, but there are also costs associated with finalizing the adoption process. Adoption is regulated provincially (so the costs may vary, depending on where you live), but the Adoption Council of Canada says the range of fees is:

- up to $3,000 for public adoption/foster care
- about $10,000 to $20,000 for adoption through a licensed private agency
- about $20,000 to $30,000 for international adoption

The federal government offers a tax credit in the tax year that the adoption is finalized, and some provinces also give tax credits for parents. Eligible adoption expenses that adoptive parents can claim are:

- fees paid to an adoption agency that's licensed by the government
- costs related to the adoption
- necessary travel and living expenses of the child and adoptive parents
- translation fees for any necessary documents

- fees paid to a foreign institution
- costs associated with the child's immigration

Planning for Multiple Babies

Two (or more) babies not only bring double (or triple) the joy and excitement, their arrival also means double the expenses — parents will need a double stroller, two car seats, an extra crib, plus double the cases of formula and packages of diapers. (If you're getting hand-me-downs, your bank account won't be hit quite as hard, but it's unlikely you'll be able to get everything you need.) There are more financial factors to consider if you're expecting multiples. Multiple Births Canada lists these as possible financial challenges:

- If you're expecting twins or triplets (or more) and are admitted to the hospital early if there are complications, and if you already have a toddler or preschooler at home, you might have to start putting money into child care earlier than you anticipated.
- Parents of multiples could have a difficult time qualifying for subsidized child care, as assistance is generally limited to very low-income families.

Vital Things to Consider in Your Budget

Life Insurance

If you have a full-time job, you probably already have group health and life insurance provided by your employer. Depending on the size of the company and your employer's plan, that coverage is probably good enough — that is, until you have a mortgage and a baby on the way.

"Those in their late twenties and early thirties are often in the stage where they have a career, they've thought about real estate — they might currently be renting and looking to buy. But when it comes to their finances, mortgages are the only real financial discussion they've likely talked about with their partner. Once they have a baby, what they need financially isn't an area they know about or have explored yet," says Kurt Rosentreter, CPA, CA.

This includes life insurance — an important area that most of us neglect when we become parents. "Group life insurance plans through employers only cover one to two times your base pay; there's never a group plan that's adequate," he says.

If you don't think you need the extra coverage, consider this: If you decide not to return to work following your parental leave and resign, or you get laid off, you'll lose your insurance. And if you don't have coverage and you pass away, your spouse or partner could be in a financial crisis, struggling to raise your baby alone and on one salary.

Contact your insurance provider to find out what's best for your growing family.

Wills

It goes without saying, no one wants to think about preparing a last will and testament right after becoming a mother or father. But now that you're responsible for another life, you have to make sure everything's in order in the event of your death. Rosentreter says that, along with a supplemental life insurance policy, getting your will made should be a top priority when you're a parent, even if you're young, healthy, and don't believe you need one.

You'll need to name someone as a guardian for your child (and any future children), designate executors and a power of attorney, and sign other legal documents that will ensure your wishes are carried out in the event that something happens to either you or both you and your partner, or if you're incapacitated in some way and are unable to care for the kids. Choosing family members is common, as is selecting different people for different responsibilities. For example, you may choose to list your parents as guardians, but opt to appoint a financially savvy aunt or uncle to handle your child's financial affairs. Don't forget to give copies of your will, power of attorney, and any other documents to the people who are listed in your plans.

Note: It is a good idea to consult a lawyer to prepare your will, as each jurisdiction in Canada has its own rules for making a will.

However, a will may legally be prepared without a lawyer with the help of a guidebook or software or by purchasing a prescribed form in an office supply store or online.

WHAT YOU WILL NEED FOR YOUR NEWBORN Sleeping	Check
approved crib	
proper crib mattress	
waterproof mattress covers	
fitted crib sheets	
receiving blankets	
thicker cotton blankets	
a firm mattress (if you choose to co-sleep with your wee one)	
Feeding — Depending on how you choose to feed your baby, you may need some or all of the following	Check
bibs and burp cloths	
breast pump (for breastfeeding and/or nursing and formula feeding)	
containers for milk storage (if pumping and saving milk)	
nursing bra and breast pads	
nursing pillow	
lanolin cream	
four- and eight-ounce bottles	
nipples (if they don't come with bottles)	
bottle liners (optional)	
formula	
sterilizer for bottles	
bottle warmer	
Hygiene and Care	
changing pad	
infant laundry detergent	

WHAT YOU WILL NEED FOR YOUR NEWBORN Cont.	Check
Hygiene and Care	
newborn-sized disposable diapers	
several dozen cloth diapers with waterproof covers (if cloth diapering)	
covered diaper pail	
wet wipes	
barrier cream (for baby's bottom to prevent and treat diaper rash)	
washcloths for baths (not to be used for diaper changes)	
infant bathtub (to place in tub or sink)	
baby soap	
hooded towels	
soft-bristled hairbrush	
infant thermometer	
infant medication to relieve fevers and teething pain	
nail scissors or clippers	
bulb syringe (used to suction mucus from baby's nose)	
Clothing	
short- and long-sleeved onesies	
short- and long-sleeved sleepers	
pants (to pair with onesies for outings)	
newborn hats	
no-scratch mittens	
socks	
sweaters and/or jackets	
snowsuit (should not be worn in the car) or bunting bag	

CHAPTER THREE

Understanding Parental Leave

JOANNE, WHO WORKS for a large communications company in Toronto, was six months pregnant when she decided it was time to chat with her human resources (HR) department about her upcoming maternity leave. Another pregnant colleague suggested she speak to her rep about how her health benefits and pension plan contributions would work during her time away.

Joanne felt she had a good handle on what she needed to know about maternity leave — she'd worked more than the required hours in the previous year to qualify, she knew she was entitled to take up to eighteen months off to spend with her new baby, and she expected to jump right back into her job (keeping both her seniority and pay grade) upon her return. So you can imagine her surprise when she asked her HR rep how the company would be paying her "top-up" — her salary (nearly $45,000) minus her employment insurance (EI) payment, so she thought — for the duration of her leave: "Will you send me cheques in the mail, or use direct deposits and just send me a paystub every two weeks?" she asked.

She says she was shocked when she found out that's not how maternity leave actually works. Instead, HR explained to Joanne that she was entitled to 100 percent of her salary for the first four weeks and

70 percent for the next two weeks. Then it got a bit more complicated — she'd then receive 70 percent of the difference between her salary and the year's maximum insurable earnings for eleven weeks. So, in total, she'd get some sort of compensation from her company for seventeen weeks, not quite the full salary she was anticipating in her planned year off.

Misconceptions About Parental Leave

Although Joanne was not going to get as much as she expected, she was lucky to receive a top-up benefit, because usually only larger companies and some unionized employers offer this bonus to employees. Joanne's story illustrates one of the biggest misconceptions there is about maternity leave. "People think their employer will provide for them, but when they start investigating, they find that many companies don't give a top-up at all — they get EI and that's it," says Rosentreter.

However, the misconceptions don't stop there. For example, soon-to-be parents don't realize that the benefits they paid for through payroll deductions (medical, dental, life and/or disability insurance) will turn into preauthorized debits from their bank account when there's no paycheque to deduct them from. Suddenly you're not getting deposits every two weeks, but you're facing bill payments.

"It's stressful enough being pregnant, but now you have to worry about money, or a lack thereof," says King. "Watch out for maternity leave — it may not be all you think. Check to see what benefits you have and how they work. There are many misconceptions out there, and people have a tendency to believe what their friends say." King recommends finding out ahead of time so you can handle the loss of income and decide how to best pay (or not pay) for those work benefits. "Don't wait. Don't get caught in the 'I have nine months to worry about that' trap. What happens if you have to go on leave early?"

The worst and arguably most common misconception by far is that folks believe their leave is when the pinch will come, when, in actuality, things really get tight when it's time to go back to work and pay for child care, or if you decide to stay home or work fewer hours.

"What happens after the baby comes? Most people don't ask themselves this question," says King. "I know a number of my friends didn't, and they were in for a big shock. They just naturally thought they would go back to work, or not. Not until it came time to really decide what was going to happen did they look at the financial consequences of their decisions." They certainly would've had time to adjust their family's finances if they'd thought about what the months after parental leave would look like.

Of course there's much more to know about maternity leave and how it can affect your finances:

- What will it mean for your household budget?
- Can you afford to live on a single salary and EI for up to a year?
- What if you're self-employed — are you entitled to any benefits?

Then there's the question of what happens when you return to work — will your maternity leave affect your potential earnings when you go back? (This phenomenon is known as the "family gap.")

We'll explore the answers to these questions, but first, let's debunk the myths and look at how maternity and parental leave work and what you need to know about EI.

How Maternity and Parental Leave Work

Let's define these terms. According to the Government of Canada, maternity leave is "an unpaid leave for eligible employees in respect to pregnancy, childbirth, post-childbirth recuperation, adoption and child care." Parental leave, also unpaid, is for eligible employees — this time male or female — who want to care for their newborn or adopted child.

By law, employers must give employees time off for maternity, parental, or adoption leave (the number of weeks you get depends on where you live; see the following table to find your province and the number of weeks you are entitled to), but your employer does not have to pay you during this time.

PROVINCE	MATERNITY LEAVE (weeks)	PARENTAL LEAVE (max weeks)
Alberta	16	62
British Columbia	17	62
Manitoba	17	63
New Brunswick	17	62
Newfoundland and Labrador	17	61
Northwest Territories	17	61
Nova Scotia	16	61
Nunavut	17	37
Ontario	17	63 (61 if maternity leave is taken)
Prince Edward Island	17	62
Quebec	18 adoption dads at birth (paternity)	52 plus 5 days for birth or
Saskatchewan	19	63 (59 if maternity/ adoption leave is taken)
Yukon	17	37

Note: Table based on data from provincial and territorial websites for one-year leave at the time of printing.

HOW THEY DO IT

Mei and Jeff welcomed their first child, a daughter, two months ago, but they started talking about what their finances would look like as a family of three prior to pregnancy. The couple decided early on that Mei would definitely take a year off and would consider taking an extended leave, depending on Jeff's business (he's self-employed). "We felt pretty prepared, actually. We discussed how our lifestyle would change. We talked about budgeting, opening an RESP, and even schooling. We also discussed employment insurance and how

---

HOW THEY DO IT Cont.

much we'd be getting monthly. We even knew how much we'd get for our Canada Child Benefit and what we'd need to do to get life insurance," says Mei. "And when we started looking into the cost of baby items, we were shocked — that stuff isn't cheap! Everything from maternity clothes to strollers to car seats to formula — it's all so expensive."

Having prepared themselves for the hit their bank account would take once they brought home their new arrival, Mei says she and Jeff have been much more mindful of their spending. "We don't go out to eat as often as we used to. We also buy a lot of used baby items as opposed to buying new. There are fewer splurges and impulse buys. We're still trying to put money into savings, and the only reason we can do it is because we spent time discussing our finances and planning well before our daughter was born."

When you're on maternity or parental leave, you're entitled as an employee to participate in some benefit plans and continue to earn time for length of service and seniority. Ontario's Ministry of Labour, for example, says employees who are off work caring for their newborn should be given their job back at the end of their leave.

What to Ask Your Employer

Remember Joanne's gaffe? Save yourself from any last-minute surprises and talk to your HR rep or your employer far in advance of your due date. Here are a few questions you might consider asking:

What happens to my remaining vacation days?
Postponing your vacation days and using them before you head back to work is quite common (plus, you'll receive your previous income but still be off work for a week or two). Find out if there are policies about using vacation days before coming back from maternity leave.

Will I get a top-up on my maternity leave benefits?
Not every company offers a top-up benefit, which pays some of your salary along with your Employment Insurance (EI) or Quebec Parental

Insurance Plan (QPIP) for a specified number of weeks. Looking at Joanne's scenario, her top-up wasn't her salary, minus EI, for fifty-two weeks. She got a percentage for seventeen weeks.

Will I still be eligible for health and dental benefits?

Some employers continue to offer full coverage while you're on leave. In other cases, if you want your benefits to continue you'll need to organize this with HR/your employer and pay the insurance premium.

Can I continue to make pension contributions?

Ask HR/your employer how you can either continue to make your contributions while you're on leave or make up for the lost contributions when you get back to work.

How will my income tax be affected?

You'll be taxed on your top-up benefit, so find out how much will be withheld while you're on leave (so you don't get a surprise tax bill at the end of the year). EI, while on maternity or parental leave, is treated like any other source of income, so the amount of tax deductions would depend on your other sources of income, says Jennifer Jones, CPA, CA. Federal and provincial or territorial taxes, where applicable, will be deducted when you receive your payments, and the government will deduct taxes based on your EI benefit rate, your province or territory, and the tax credits you indicate you are entitled to at the time of your application, says Vivian Leung, CPA, CA. You'll receive a T4E slip that you must report on your tax return.

How Employment Insurance Works

EI Maternity Benefits

When it comes to EI, maternity benefits are offered to biological mothers (this includes surrogates) who can't work because they're either expecting or have just given birth. (Maternity benefits cannot be shared between parents.) These benefits can be followed by parental benefits, which are offered to mothers or fathers who are caring for a new baby or newly adopted child. A maximum of fifteen weeks of maternity benefits are offered. You can start collecting EI maternity benefits twelve weeks before your due date and they end as late as seventeen weeks after the birth. To receive benefits, you need to sign a statement declaring either the date you expect to give birth or the date of the birth.

EI Parental Benefits

Parents can choose between standard parental benefits or extended parental benefits. Your choice determines the number of weeks and the weekly amount you'll receive. With standard parental benefits, you can take up to forty weeks (but one parent cannot receive more than thirty-five weeks); with extended parental benefits, you can take up to sixty-nine weeks (but one parent cannot receive more than sixty-one weeks). This time can be taken by one parent or can be split between both parents. If sharing the benefits, each parent must choose the same option and submit their own applications. Parents can receive their weeks of benefits at the same time or one after another. (Note: You don't get more time if you have twins or triplets, or if you adopt more than one infant or child at the same time.)

EI benefits start when your weekly earnings are reduced by more than 40 percent due to pregnancy or your need to care for a new baby.

There are several ways you can use your standard parental benefits. Here are a few examples:

- If one parent chooses to take ten weeks of standard parental benefits before going back to work, the other parent can use the remaining thirty weeks of standard parental benefits.
- If the biological mother wants to go back to work after her maternity leave is up, the other parent can then take the forty weeks of standard parental benefits.
- If one parent chooses to go back to work after taking a few weeks of standard parental benefits, then realizes he or she would prefer to stay at home with their little one, he or she is still entitled to the unused weeks of standard parental benefits, as long as the fifty-two-week period after the birth or adoption placement hasn't expired.

Here are a few examples of how you can use your extended parental benefits:

- If the biological mother wants to go back to work after her maternity leave, the other parent can take the sixty-one weeks of extended parental benefits.
- If one parent chooses to take twenty weeks of extended parental benefits before going back to work, the other parent can use the remaining forty-nine weeks of extended parental benefits.
- If one parent chooses to go back to work after taking a few weeks of extended parental benefits, then realizes he or she would rather stay home with their little one, he or she is still entitled to the unused weeks of extended parental benefits, as long as the seventy-eight-week period after the birth or adoption placement hasn't expired.

Eligibility

To be eligible to get EI benefits, you must have paid EI premiums (i.e., be employed in insurable employment) and have accumulated six hundred hours of insurable employment in the fifty-two weeks before the start of your claim. (There isn't a minimum number of hours you have to work to be eligible for the Quebec Parental Insurance Plan, but you must have $2,000 in insurable income in the year prior to receiving benefits.) You'll need to have paid the maximum amount on EI premiums on all earnings. For example, for every $100 earned in 2020, your employer deducts $1.58, until your earnings reach the maximum yearly insurable amount (which is $54,200), which means the maximum amount of EI premiums paid in 2020 is $856.36 per year. (In Quebec, which handles its own parental benefits, for every $100 earned $1.20 is deducted, up to a yearly maximum of $650.40.)

Applying for EI

You'll need to apply for EI so Service Canada can assess what you're entitled to receive. Make sure to apply at the time you stop working (even if this is before your employer has sent you your Record of Employment, which you can always submit later). You could lose benefits if you apply more than four weeks after your final day of work.

You can go online (servicecanada.gc.ca) to apply for maternity benefits; here's what you'll need:

- your social insurance number (SIN)
- your mother's maiden name
- your mailing and residential addresses
- your banking information (including the financial institution's name and number, branch number, and your account number)
- your expected due date

When you apply for parental benefits, you'll need this information:

- the birth date of your child (or, in the case of adoption, the date your child was placed with you)
- your partner's SIN (if you're sharing benefits)
- your employer's name and address (any employers you've worked for in the past year — if you've been fired from or quit a job within that time, you must explain the facts and provide start and end dates)
- the dates and earnings for your highest paid weeks of insurable earnings in the past year (this information is used to calculate your EI rate)

You can apply for maternity benefits and parental benefits at the same time. You will need to submit all your records of employment issued to you in the last fifty-two weeks. If your employer issued you an electronic ROE, a copy would have been sent directly to Service Canada by your employer, so you don't need to provide copies to Service Canada. If your employer issued paper ROEs, you must request copies of all ROEs issued to you in the past fifty-two weeks and send them to Service Canada as soon as possible after you submit your EI application.

If you're eligible for EI, you'll get your first payment within four weeks of the date your application and documents are received. Keep in mind that there's a waiting period before your EI will kick in — it's called the "one-week wait," and it often comes as a surprise to new parents. We'll talk about this later.

What You'll Receive
If You Choose to Take the Standard Twelve Months

Most people get 55 percent of their average insurable weekly salary, up to a certain amount. In 2020, for example, the maximum yearly insurable earnings amount was $54,200, which means you would receive a maximum of $573 per week. Don't forget EI is taxable, so federal and provincial or territorial taxes will be deducted from this amount. Leung says it's important to remember that the amount deducted by the government may not be accurate, and if you think the government has not deducted enough, you should put some money aside for when you file your tax return.

Your benefits will stop when you've received all the weeks you're entitled to or the maximum period has been reached — maternity benefits end seventeen weeks after your expected birth date or the week you give birth, and EI standard parental benefits end fifty-two weeks after the week your child was born (fifty-five weeks if you are sharing your parental benefits with your partner).

If You Choose to Take the Extended Eighteen Months

The government made changes in the 2017 federal budget allowing extended parental leave of up to eighteen months (however, the amount you receive from EI per month is lower). Instead of receiving 55 percent of your average insurable weekly salary, if you opt for eighteen months' leave, extended parental benefits are paid at a weekly benefit rate of 33 percent of your average weekly insurable earnings, up to a maximum amount. For 2020, you can receive a maximum amount of $344 per week for up to sixty-one weeks.

EI for Self-Employed Parents

According to Statistics Canada, in 2018 there were nearly 2.9 million self-employed people in the country — a number that's been growing steadily.

Self-employed new parents are also entitled to EI benefits, including maternity benefits (for mothers who give birth; these benefits cover the time surrounding the birth for up to fifteen weeks) and parental benefits (for any parent to care for his or her newborn or newly adopted child or children).

You must register online with the Canada Employment Insurance Commission to participate in EI (www.canada.ca/en/employment-social-development/corporate/portfolio/ei-commission.html). You'll need a My Service Canada Account (you can access online at www.canada.ca/en/employment-social-development/services/my-account.html or at Service Canada Centre kiosks). Click on "Access My Service Canada Account" and follow the instructions. After you register, Service Canada will mail you a personal access code. If you already have an access code, just log in with your code and password, then select "Employment Insurance for the Self-Employed" to register.

Note: In order to apply for EI special benefits, you have to wait one year from the date of your confirmed registration.

What You Need Before You Start

To apply for EI special benefits, you'll need to complete an online application for EI benefits. You'll also need the following information:

- your social insurance number (SIN)
- your mother's maiden name
- your mailing and residential addresses
- your banking information (including the financial institution's name and number, branch number, and your account number)

EI Benefit Statement

After filing your EI application, you'll be mailed an EI benefit statement. With this paperwork you'll get your four-digit access code (it's printed in the shaded area at the top of the benefit statement).

This code is used to identify you; it ensures your confidentiality, and it's needed to submit your required biweekly reports and to get information about your claim. It goes without saying, but don't share this code, as you'll be held responsible if someone accesses your information or modifies your claim without your knowing. The government suggests storing your access code separately from your social insurance number.

Payment of EI Premiums

When you receive notification that your registration was successful, your EI premiums will be calculated based on your income tax and benefit return for that year. So if you registered in 2021 to participate in this program, your EI premiums will be calculated based on your 2021 tax and benefit return and will be payable by April 30, 2022. After that, if you pay your income tax by installments to the Canada Revenue Agency (CRA), your premiums may be included in your installment payments. Regardless of when you register, EI premiums are payable based on your self-employed income for the entire year.

You'll receive your payments via direct deposit. EI payments are deposited automatically into your bank account two business days after your EI report is processed.

Calculation of EI Premiums

EI premiums are calculated by the CRA, and they are based on your self-employed earnings. For example, in 2020, for every $100 you earned, you'd need to contribute $1.58 in EI premiums up to a maximum of $856.36 (this is the same amount that employees pay). Quebec has its own parental insurance program that offers maternity and parental leave. Self-employed people in Quebec pay $1.20 for every $100 of earnings up to a total of $650.40 for the year. The good news is you will not have to pay the employer's portion of the EI premium.

Eligibility

After you've registered and waited twelve months from the date of your confirmed registration, you'll qualify for EI special benefits if:

- you've reduced the amount of time you devote to your business by more than 40 percent because:
- your child was born

- you're caring for your newborn or adopted child or children
- you've earned a minimum amount of self-employed earnings during the calendar year preceding the year you submit a claim. (For example, for 2020, you need to have earned at least $7,279 in 2019.)
- for EI maternity or parental benefit claims specifically, you've provided the expected date of birth of the child and/or the actual birth date once the baby is born, or the official placement date if adopting a child

What You'll Receive

The weekly benefit amount is 55 percent of your average weekly earnings from the calendar year before you submit an application for EI special benefits. These earnings are your total self-employment income minus any losses (as calculated according to the *Income Tax Act*) divided by fifty-two. Note: The amount of your benefits may decrease if you're continuing to work or if your business generates earnings while you're collecting EI.

HOW THEY DO IT
Before they had their first daughter, eight-month-old Allie, most of Megan and Roy's money was spent on vacations. "We'd save up all year and usually go away between Christmas and New Year's when Roy was off school. Other than that, and spending money ordering in, we really didn't go out much, preferring to spend our time at home together watching TV and playing video games," Megan says.

Working on finishing his accounting certification, Roy was adamant that he and Megan dive deep into their finances prior to planning a baby. "We really looked at everything, especially what I'd be bringing in while on maternity leave. That was Roy's main concern and what we focused on most. He created an Excel spreadsheet with all of our typical monthly expenses and what we both bring in with our salaries." Before getting pregnant, after all their monthly bills were paid they were able to save a small amount from every paycheque. "But when we starting planning, we calculated what my monthly income would be using an online maternity leave calculator to check if we'd be able to afford to cover our mortgage and all of our bills," she says. "We also compared what it would be like if I took the one-year versus eighteen-month leave, taking daycare payments into consideration."

Megan applied for employment insurance right away, and even though they had done the research and knew what it would mean for their bank account, that first payment still came as a shock. "EI isn't a lot. It's half my pay. If I chose the eighteen-month leave, it would've been a third of my pay. Money has been super tight for us. At this point we're not saving anything — we're definitely spending more than we're bringing in. Whatever we receive goes right back into our monthly expenses. The Canada Child Benefit is helping with our bills. I'd love to save that money in an account for Allie, but right now we really need it as part of my salary. Hopefully once I go back to work we can start saving those payments."

Money has been so tight that Roy decided to pick up a side hustle — he's a food delivery driver and is able to pick up shifts when he has downtime. "The idea for the second job came one night when we ordered fast food delivery just after Allie was born. We started talking about what the job entails and, out of curiosity, it led Roy to apply right there on the spot. He got his first shift a week later," Megan says. "He always talked about getting another job on the side for pocket money, but he didn't want it to take time away from us. This job allows him to pick his own schedule — most of his shifts are after Allie's bedtime — and he can be home if there aren't any orders coming in. It really helps cover expenses, and the additional income has ensured we don't dip into our savings account too often."

Working While on EI

The government knows you may need to work and/or your business may continue to generate income while you're receiving special benefits. You must always declare on your biweekly report all of your earnings from your work or any earnings your business generates while you're receiving EI special benefits. For anything you earn while receiving EI, you can keep fifty cents of your benefits for every dollar you earn, up to

90 perent of your previous weekly earnings. Money earned above that amount is deducted on a dollar-for-dollar basis.

You can find more information on EI special benefits for self-employed people at www.canada.ca/en/services/benefits/ei/ei-self-employed-workers. html and www.canada.ca/en/employment-social-development/programs/ei/ ei-list/working-while-claim.html.

EI: The One-Week Wait

As previously mentioned, before your EI benefits kick in, there's a one-week wait during which you won't be paid. Think of the one-week wait as a deductible for your benefits. You'll want to make sure you have some extra money in the bank to cover you while you wait, which could be a challenge for many parents.

A 2015 study conducted by the Chartered Professional Accountants of Canada (CPA Canada) asked folks how they would come up with $500 if an unforeseen emergency expense came up: 43 percent of respondents said they'd need to use their credit card and 27 percent said they'd use their line of credit or a bank loan.

In another CPA Canada study in 2016, respondents were asked why they don't have an emergency savings fund. Half (51 percent) simply said it was because they don't earn enough, they're on disability, they're a student, or they're unemployed. (The situation is even worse for millennials in their thirties and generation X in their forties — 55 percent and 51 percent respectively would struggle.) Plus, 41 percent of employees end up spending all or more of their net pay due to higher living costs, and 22 percent said they wouldn't be able to come up with just $2,000 within one month if they had an emergency expense.

What's more, a 2018 study conducted by the Canadian Payroll Association found nearly half (48 percent) of working Canadians surveyed would find it hard to meet their financial obligations if their paycheque were delayed by one week.

Now that you know it's coming, be sure to sock away a bit of extra cash, if possible, to get you through this waiting period.

Parental Leave and Your Budget

The odds are that new parents — whether you're single or a couple — have probably never considered how their finances will change after a baby enters the picture or the type of financial planning that needs to be explored when their family grows.

"For two professionals who have no children and lots of free cash flow, things are about to get a lot tighter," Rosentreter says. "Your finances bottleneck when it comes time for maternity leave." This is the time when you'll need some kind of a budget. If you and your significant other aren't on the same page, it can affect your relationship, especially if one of you is a spender and the other is a saver.

If you're not yet pregnant but still contemplating pregnancy, now's a good time to step back to do some strategic thinking. Accountants and financial advisers are third-party resources who can offer a second opinion and relieve some of the stress of trying to figure out the numbers on your own.

There's no doubt you'll get all kinds of advice about how to rein in your spending once you're on maternity leave and potentially go from a dual- to a single-income household, but if you haven't already given birth, your best bet is to start practising early.

Analyze Your Cash Flow

Don't worry — this sounds much more daunting than it is. If you're not already doing it, start tracking how you spend your hard-earned cash. Use the following guide to analyze your cash flow.

Over twelve months, write down:

- Basic expenses: These are "needs" (as opposed to "wants"). They include your mortgage or rent, utilities, insurance payments, debt repayment (including line of credit payments), RRSP contributions, medical or dental care, property taxes, transportation costs, groceries, and clothing.
- Other expenses: These are your "wants," and they include extra clothing, meals out at restaurants, manicures and pedi-

cures, trips to Starbucks, entertainment, gifts, vacations, etc. New moms might also want to put money aside for postpartum exercise groups (classes like Strollerfit allow you to get out with your wee one, meet other new moms, and get in a workout, which can not only work wonders physically but also really be beneficial for mothers who are suffering from the baby blues or postpartum depression). There are lots of mommy-and-me or daddy-and-me groups parents can join, and not all of them are free (a typical community-based group in Toronto, for example, costs about $100 for about eight weeks).

FINANCIAL TIP

"Blue-sky the range of possibilities. Start by writing down your financial goals, which might include things like owning a home, having kids, buying cars, putting aside funds for a retirement nest egg. If you're not financially savvy, get an adviser — this will give you a perspective on the number of kids you could financially manage, how far apart you can have them to properly support them, the quality of your retirement, etc."

— Kurt Rosentreter, CPA, CA

FINANCIAL TIP

"I started budgeting when I found out I was pregnant. Luckily, I had my husband supporting the household when I was off, and we didn't have to dip into our savings much. However, given that our total monthly cash flow dropped, I'd say by 30 percent, we avoided eating out too much, we travelled during a less busy season, and we didn't spend too much on the baby, other than the regular equipment we needed, such as our car seat and high chair."

— Han Shu, CPA, CA

Using a template from the internet or creating your own budget sheet (like the one linked at the end of this chapter) will help give you an idea of what you can trim from your spending. Want to save some cash before baby arrives? Make your daily caramel macchiato a once-a-week treat, or turn pizza Fridays into homemade pizza Fridays. You won't be able to cut the things you *need*, but you can work on trimming your *wants*. Remember, "This is not the year you're going to Tanzania to look at elephants," says Rosentreter.

Next, do a little forecasting and calculate how much you'll get from the government for EI, Canada Child Benefit (CCB), and any provincial benefits (see Chapter 5), as well as the income of the parent who will be working (if there is one), and see if the kind of spending you did in the past year will fit comfortably below that income. You're likely to find you'll need to make adjustments to your spending habits, so it makes sense to test drive your new budget and to practise living on that amount to see how you manage.

When it comes down to it, it's best to plan in advance and budget, but don't get too hung up on what your finances will look like when you're on parental leave. The truth is, it's when it's time to return to work and budget for the cost of child care that you'll really need to keep an eye on your pennies.

FINANCIAL TIP

"If you've never done a budget before, a good starting point is to look at your spending over the past year to get a sense of your average spending. Summarize your spending across major categories, such as rent, food, transportation, clothing, vacations, etc. Once you understand what you spend your money on, you can develop a budget for once the baby arrives. Your spending patterns may change, so take those changes into account as best you can."

— Jennifer Jones, CPA, CA

The Family Gap

We've already looked at the cost of baby equipment, diapers, formula, etc., and we'll look at child care costs in the next chapter. But there's something else that could put a damper on your finances. The "family gap" (also known as the "motherhood gap" or "child penalty") is a well-documented phenomenon that new parents (and specifically new mothers) encounter. This penalty measures (with all other factors being equal) how much the earnings of women who have children fall below those who don't have children.

According to a Canadian Research Data Centre Network study published in *Canadian Public Policy* in September 2013, the wage gap is about 40 percent in both the year a woman gives birth and the following year (the estimated salary loss is about $11,000 the birth year and $8,000 the year after). The study suggests that it isn't until seven years after a woman gives birth that the child penalty disappears. In 2009, Statistics Canada also found that forty-year-old childless women earned almost 30 percent more than mothers who had taken three years off for maternity leaves. In 2011, Statistics Canada discovered women who had kids earned about 12 to 20 percent less than women without kids.

Another study that TD Economics conducted, called Career Interrupted — The Economic Impact of Motherhood, found that mothers experience wage penalties "each time they exit and re-enter the workforce." In 2010 when this research was released, there was a 3 percent wage penalty per year of absence from their jobs. The authors estimated that a woman who works for six years at a $64,000-per-year job, takes three years to raise her kids, then returns to her job to work full-time for twenty years would lose more than $300,000 over the course of her career.

Another factor of the motherhood wage gap is that women have a greater responsibility at home after a child is born, which some employers see as a change in their employees' priorities. (Employers believe many absences are signs that women aren't committed to their jobs. Plus, mothers may become less responsive to job incentives such as salary increases and more attracted to work/life balance.)

Mothers who have experienced this gap cite the following complaints:

- Some feel as if they're "out of sight and out of mind" to employers, who forget about moving them up in the company.
- Many say they didn't receive a salary increase (even a modest cost-of-living increase, which can end up being a couple of thousand dollars a year) when they were on maternity leave.

- Many say it's hard to get back into the workforce if you are restructured out of your job during maternity leave or take extra time off to be with the kids before going back to work.

Budget Template

To access and complete your own budget worksheet, please visit cpacanada.ca/finlitresources, under money management worksheets, to download your own excel spreadsheet.

CHAPTER FOUR

Planning for Child Care

DO YOU KNOW these surprising facts about life in Canada?

- There are more than two million caribou roaming around the country,
- Eighty percent of the world's maple syrup supply comes from Canada,
- Pekwachnamaykoskwaskwaypinwanik Lake has more letters in its name than any other place in Canada, and
- If you live in Toronto and have an infant in full-time child care, you're looking at an average cost of — wait for it — more than $21,000 annually.

If you haven't already investigated the cost of child care in your area, and if you live in a big city, do yourself a favour and take this advice: be prepared for major sticker shock!

In 2019, the Canadian Centre for Policy Alternatives (CCPA) published a report (aptly titled *Developmental Milestones: Childcare Fees in Canada's Big Cities 2018*) about the cost of daycare services in twenty-eight cities across the country, and the results were alarming. Yes, there's plenty to consider besides the price of daycare — things like convenience, quality, and availability — but the cost can make or break your plans, even though child care expenses you incur are deductible on your income tax return.

"Child care expenses incurred in order for parents to earn active income, such as employment income, is deductible," says Shu. Generally, the partner with the lower net income claims child care expenses. (This person can receive a maximum deduction of $8,000 annually for a child younger than age seven and $5,000 for a child aged seven to fifteen). If both parents have equal net incomes, you have to agree on which one of you will claim child care expenses. (For more information on who should claim child care, search child care expenses on Canada.ca and click on Line 21400 — child care expenses.)

Child care expenses are the amounts you or another person (spouse, partner, etc.) have paid to have someone look after an eligible child so that you or another person can:

- earn income from employment
- conduct business either alone or as an active partner
- go to school under the conditions identified under educational program
- carry on research or similar work, for which you or the other person received a grant

Child care expenses can only be claimed for an eligible child. An eligible child is:

- your or your spouse's or common-law partner's child, or
- a child who was dependent on you or your spouse or common-law partner, and whose net income in 2019 was $12,069 or less

The child has to have been younger than sixteen years old at some time in the year.

Types of child care expenses could include payments made to:

- caregivers who provided child care services
- daycare centres or day nursery schools

- educational institutions, for the part of the fees that relate specifically to child care services
- day sports schools or day camps where the primary goal of the camp is to care for kids
- boarding schools, overnight sports schools, or camps where lodging is involved

You can't claim payments for:

- clothing, transportation costs, or medical or hospital care
- fees that relate to education costs at an educational institution, such as tuition fees for a regular program or a sports study program
- fees for leisure or recreational activities, such as tennis lessons or the annual registration for Scouts

You'll find there are several types of child care placements available, and it's possible to find less expensive alternatives to daycare centres. Still, it's most likely the biggest expense you'll be faced with after your little one arrives and you're ready to go back to work.

In addition to any personal choices about whether to stay home after your child's birth or return to work, the price of child care means you should do some calculations before your parental leave comes to a halt. Does going back to your full-time job make financial sense for you and your new family? You'll find more on this in Chapter 7.

Eventually you'll find yourself weighing the pros and cons of going back to the daily grind and paying for daycare (including the price of gas, parking, public transit fees, lunches out, clothing, etc.) or staying at home with your baby but forfeiting your salary. Your decision will depend not only on your finances but on whether you love your work and wish to maintain your seniority and career progression, and whether or not you feel being a stay-at-home parent is for you. You might also choose to investigate the ways you can return to work and save money on daycare by telecommuting or job sharing.

Here's what you need to know about how child care is set up in Canada before you make a decision.

How Child Care Works

Child care is provincially regulated, and nearly all paid child care (there are slight variations, depending on your province) falls into one of two categories — licensed and unlicensed (we discuss these options on the next page). There are also three main types of care:

- full-time daycare for infants (younger than eighteen months)
- full-day care for toddlers (up to three years old)
- full-day preschool care (three to five years old)

Note: Some provinces use different age ranges. For example, infant rooms in Saskatchewan take babies from six weeks to thirty months, while the range in both Manitoba and Newfoundland is up to twenty-four months.

Later, when your child starts kindergarten, there are before- and after-school programs available through daycare centres and schools. These are also provincially regulated.

PARENT'S TIP

"Start searching as early as possible! Whether you're planning to go back to work right after your parental leave or you are considering taking extra time off, make sure you're visiting and interviewing daycare providers. In some big cities, spaces are limited and spots can fill up well before babies cut their first tooth."

— Alex, mom of three

PARENT'S TIP

"If both parents need to go back to work, it's important to visit a couple of daycares. Compare the cost, facility, online reviews, qualifications of the teachers, etc. Leave sufficient time to allow gradual entry for the baby so he or she is well transitioned into a new routine and environment."

— Han, mom of one

Licensed Child Care

These daycare centres are regulated and inspected regularly by the province to ensure they're kept operating up to provincial standards. Depending on the number of staff and educators, it's possible for a centre to care for more than one hundred kids at a time. Some home child care providers are also licensed and can hold two to twelve kids, depending on the province's regulations.

Unlicensed Child Care

If you're considering going the daycare centre route, you're almost guaranteed you'll have a licensed provider (all centre-based care should be licensed), but if you choose unlicensed home daycare, know that there are no regulations that need to be followed, except for the number of children allowed in the daycare (anyone who cares for more than five children has to be licensed). These locations are legal, but they're not inspected, and authorities only get involved in checking out the daycare location if complaints are made.

What It's Going to Cost You

Daycare Centres

Here's some good news before getting down to the details: Generally, the older children get, the less expensive their care gets. It makes sense that rates are higher for the infant group because babies require more attention and infant rooms need more staff than other age groups. If you or your partner take a year off, depending on where you live, you'll likely have to pay the higher prices for just six months. If you return to work before your baby is a year old, you'll be paying a premium until they reach eighteen months.

Note: See the chart at the end of this chapter for average fees in the twenty-eight cities studied by the CCPA.

Vicky, a mother of two in Ottawa, says her family has tried many different arrangements for child care, including co-ops, Montessori, and non-profits.

"We chose care based on the age of the kids, availability, and proximity. Finding and paying for child care has been the biggest stress and caused the most worry for us."

The least expensive option she found was a parent-run co-op, "but not if you include my lost wages for the days I was on duty and the hours of work it took to run," she adds. "The most expensive care we had was a private, for-profit Montessori school — we paid $23,000 for two kids one year and still didn't have coverage for professional activity (PA) days and in the summer. We now use an extended daycare program at school for both kids. It's still almost $600 per month, plus PA days, March Break, and summer."

Vicky says she would have opted for a not-for-profit centre for toddler and preschooler care, but there isn't one available in her neighbourhood.

PARENT'S TIP

"Home daycare costs us $42 per day for our two-and-a-half-year-old and $48 per day for our nine-month-old."

— Pam, mom of two

PARENT'S TIP

"I'm looking at full-time infant daycare spots — at centres, not home daycares — and the range is $1,300 to $1,800 on the low end, $2,100 to $2,400 on the high end. The price drops considerably — to $950 per month — after your child is old enough for the toddler room at eighteen months."

— Paul, dad of one

According to the 2018 Canadian Centre for Policy Alternatives study, the priciest daycares for babies younger than twenty-four months are for-profit centres in Toronto, where parents can expect to pay an average of $1,685 each month. (That's more than $10,000 for six months of care! It would also be a good amount of money to put into an RESP or RRSP or toward your mortgage or next car.) Mississauga, ON, is next in line with monthly fees of $1,591, and Kitchener, ON, ranks third most expensive with monthly fees of $1,495. On the other side of Canada, folks in Vancouver can expect to pay about $1,400 each month, and those in Halifax are looking at an average of $967 per month. Note: This price usually includes healthy, hot lunches, as well as fun programming such as art and music. Be sure to ask about this when you visit centres.

The least expensive is every city and town in Quebec, thanks to the cap of $8.25 per day (in 2019) the provincial government put on child care fees. (Parents in Toronto, for example, pay about ten times more than parents in Montreal for the same services.)

Toddler daycare is slightly less expensive. Parents in Toronto are paying about $1,367 per month for care, and those in Vancouver can expect to pay about $1,407 per month. If you're in Quebec (which caps services at $7.75 each day), you'll generally spend less, about $190 per month. Not surprisingly, Toronto also ranks most expensive in preschooler care, which costs an average of $1,150 per month, while parents in Vancouver, Calgary, Vaughan, Ottawa, and London (the last three in Ontario) all pay about $1,000. Those in Halifax can expect to pay about $867 per month; parents in Saskatoon pay about $730 a month; and Edmonton folks will pay about $835 each month.

Home-Based Daycare

It's tough to put a specific fee on home-based child care, as several factors affect the price. First, location plays a huge part (as we've seen from the price of daycare centres); you can expect to pay significantly more for care if you're in a major city. Next, the fee depends on the number of kids in the home and what the provider offers. For example, you're looking at a premium if you expect a weekly menu (featuring healthy, hot lunches) and certain educational programs (music, art, etc.).

Live-In or Live-Out Nannies

Live-in and live-out nannies are gaining in popularity because they are often a less expensive option for new parents and for those who have more than one child. If you have the room for an extra person in your home, room and board account for most of a nanny's fees. You could be looking at up to about $600 per week for a live-out nanny who works full-time at your home. Cooperative arrangements are also a good choice to save money. If you have friends in your neighbourhood who also need care, consider going in together on child care and you are more likely to get a better rate.

While the cost of hiring a trustworthy live-in nanny is definitely attractive to many parents, it's important to create an employment contract. You can find a sample you can print and fill out on the government's website (www.canada.ca/en/immigration-refugees-citizen ship/services/work-canada/hire-foreign-worker/caregiver-program/ eligible.html). This contract includes a list of everyone who lives in the home, the duration of the contract, and the responsibilities and duties that the employee will be required to fulfill. Of course, the nanny's primary job will be to care for your little one (be sure to mark down the times and days you expect him or her to work — for example, 8:00 a.m. to 5:30 p.m., Monday to Friday), but you might decide he or she will also assist with light housekeeping, the baby's laundry, perhaps some meal preparation, etc., so make sure these tasks are listed on the contract. You'll also need to fill out rate of pay, vacation and sick day allowances, as well as overtime hours, in accordance with provincial or territorial labour and employment standards. (You must also pay the nanny for provincial, territorial, and national statutory and public holidays.)

When it comes to your taxes, be aware that your contract stipulates that you agree to pay taxes and submit all deductions payable (this includes employment insurance, income tax, Canada Pension Plan or Quebec Pension Plan, etc.). Don't forget to ask your caregiver for his or her social insurance number or business identification number — you'll need it to claim your expenses on your tax return.

Other Options

If you have parents or other family helping with child care, consider yourself lucky. You'll rest easy knowing your little one is with those you love and trust. Depending on their availability, your parents or relatives might not be able to watch your child every day. In that case, you'll likely need to put your tot in daycare on a part-time basis. Some believe this gives your child the best of both worlds — he or she will get to spend time with family and socialize with other kids on alternate days.

Be aware that not all daycares offer part-time spots, so you'll need to confirm before booking.

Daycare and Safety

Whether you're sending your child to a daycare centre or home-based daycare, or you're bringing in a live-in or live-out nanny, it's vital for you to cross a few must-dos off your list: you'll need to visit the centre, prepare a list of questions to ask the provider, and check references.

When you visit a daycare centre or home-based centre, look for a clean, safe environment. Watch the other children play and see how the employees engage and deal with little ones. You'll get a good sense of the atmosphere if you sit quietly and just observe. Note from the Canadian Paediatric Society: If you visit home-based daycares and you're told that unannounced parent drop-ins aren't permitted (you might hear it's because it's disruptive to children), cross these providers off your list.

Make sure you're prepared with a list of questions. Any provider you meet with should give you ample time to ask as many questions as you're comfortable with. Here are several you might consider adding to your list:

- Are you licensed and/or supervised by an agency?
- What are your qualifications? What are your staff's qualifications?
- Have you and your staff had first aid training?
- Have you and your staff had police checks?
- How many staff members do you have, and are there other people who will have access to my child?
- Can parents drop in unannounced to see their child?
- What is your late pickup fee?
- Do you have a waiting list?
- What holidays do you take off?
- What is your illness policy?
- What is your vacation policy?
- How do you discipline children?

- Do you have separate areas for play and naps (indoor play, outdoor play, nap area)?
- What activities do you offer?
- What snacks and meals do you serve?
- Is this a smoke-free facility/home?

Before you decide which centre or provider you're going with, do your due diligence and check references. Instead of simply looking at the list of references you'll no doubt be handed, take it a step further and speak to other parents who use the same centre or provider. Ask them about their experiences, their child's health and happiness, etc. The same goes for nannies if you're going that route. Ask lots of questions when interviewing and request the names and numbers of a few parents whom you can speak with.

PARENT'S TIP

"Do some research and find out what the rules are for licensed and unlicensed daycares in your province or territory. (If you're only interested in licensed daycares, look for the display decals that identify a centre or home-based facility as licensed by the government; that's how it works in Ontario — check your provincial or territorial child care legislation rules to find out what to look for in your city.) Rules include whether, for example, home-based providers need to include their own children in the number of kids they're allowed to have in their home, as well as the maximum number of children younger than two who are permitted. (In Ontario, licensed providers can only care for a maximum of six children under the age of thirteen; unlicensed child care providers can care for a maximum of five children under the age of thirteen.) Both licensed and unlicensed providers have to give you receipts for their services."

— Jacqueline, mom of three

PARENT'S TIP

"We paid $1,800 for infant care, $1,500 for toddler, and $1,054 for preschool and got prepared, hot food."

— Carter, dad of two

PARENT'S TIP

"We did a nanny share, which was about $300 a week for four days a week. We now have amazing home care — it's $1,500 a month for the baby for four days a week and $360 for after-school care, for a total of $1,860 per month. If I had to pay for five days a week, it would cost us $2,230 per month."

— Melanie, mom of two

PARENT'S TIP

"We chose this centre because of the location and the lack of other options in our area. We pay $710 per month for three days a week for our two-year-old. I'm that lucky mom who has parents and in-laws who watch my kid the other two days a week, so I can still justify having a full-time job."

— Whitney, mom of two

PROVINCIAL SUBSIDY PROGRAMS FOR LOW-INCOME FAMILIES

Most provinces offer daycare subsidies for low-income families. Amounts vary by the number and ages of your children. The table below, from the 2016 CCPA report, *A Growing Concern: 2016 Child Care Fees in Canada's Big Cities*, shows how much a two-parent family with one school-aged child and one preschooler, plus an after-tax income less than $30,823, would pay for a subsidized child care spot in major cities across the country. Note: Outside of Quebec, waitlists for subsidized child care placements may be very long.

PE: Charlottetown
This family would pay $144 per month.

NB: Saint John
This family would pay $193 per month.

NS: Halifax
This family would pay $391 per month.

NL: St. John's
This family would pay $119 per month.

PROVINCIAL SUBSIDY PROGRAMS FOR LOW-INCOME FAMILIES Cont.
ON: Most cities in Ontario This family would pay $90 per month.
MB: Winnipeg This family would pay $279 per month.
SK: Saskatoon This family would pay $497 per month.
AB: Calgary This family would pay $478 per month.
BC: Vancouver This family would pay $353 per month.

Should You Go Back to Work or Stay Home?

This is the million-dollar question for many on parental leave. You will have days when you couldn't imagine leaving your precious offspring to head back to work, and you will certainly have others when you're so tired of the feed-diaper-feed-diaper-nap-feed routine that you can't wait to get back to the place where you have freedom (at least at lunch hour) and the ability to engage your mind and connect with other adults. This is not an easy question to answer, and there is no one perfect answer for every situation.

"For some families, having a stay-at-home parent is more feasible. There are also families where two incomes are needed to support the household. It's not easy to send an eleven-month-old to a strange environment like daycare," says Shu. "In my situation, where both parents are working full-time, we really make sure we each spend a good amount of quality time with our baby. For instance, every day when I come home from work, I make sure I devote 100 percent of my attention and time to the baby. In these hours I don't keep my cellphone around, no emails, no laptop. Just me playing with my baby. The same goes for my husband. When both parents work outside the home they're still capable of giving kids a secure childhood."

In households where it might be an option, new parents have to look at the income the stay-at-home parent was earning while working versus the cost of child care — that can change dramatically depending on where you live and how much you earn. Some parents opt to arrange their work schedules so that one parent is always at home. This can be challenging, but it's doable. For example, if your monthly take-home pay leaves you with just a few bucks after you've paid for daycare, it may make more sense for you to stay at home (if this is a possibility in your home and an arrangement you're interested in). Don't forget that if you add to your family later, daycare for two or more children will be doubled, tripled, etc.

The Pros and Cons of Going Back to Work

There are obviously pros and cons to going back into the workforce. At the top of the list of pros is quite an important financial reason: the ability to have a higher disposable income. There are also things like more earned RRSP contribution room, pension and group RRSP contributions, increased income later in life, social contact with peers, the allure of a challenging career, and a better chance of overall financial stability. One of the biggest financial impacts would be the ability to save for retirement and meet current day-to-day expenses. Long-term career development is also key for many women, and studies have shown that taking leave can affect a mom's earnings and career advancement, which we mentioned back in Chapter 3.

The cons are also important to consider. These include: added stress around your schedule (e.g. daycare pickup by a certain time, taking days off when your child is sick), less time spent with your child and family, and, of course, the high cost of child care.

You might also be interested in knowing another key figure before making your decision — the CCPA also looked at the percentage of a mother's income that goes toward child care in their 2014 report, *The Parent Trap: Child Care Fees in Canada's Big Cities*. At the time, women who lived in Ontario (especially in Kitchener, Hamilton, Mississauga, Windsor, London, Brampton, and Toronto) spent about a third of their paycheques on daycare. (It was the same story in Surrey and St. John's.)

Mothers in Saskatoon, Edmonton, Calgary, Halifax, and Vancouver ended up using about a quarter of their salary, while those in Winnipeg, Montreal, Quebec City, Laval, and Gatineau saved the most on daycare. (Quebecers spent only 4 to 6 percent on child care.)

Many experts agree there's no right or wrong answer to this huge question, and you'll need to weigh not having an income and saving on daycare against the cost of going back to work. One thing you can try, according to some financial experts, is to live on one income for as long as you can before you have your baby.

Coming up with and pitching alternative work arrangements (telecommuting, job sharing, etc.) to your company is gaining in popularity, as organizations are realizing the importance of work/life balance. Read more about the most common arrangements in Chapter 7.

FINANCIAL TIP

"In trying to decide what to do (whether to return to work or stay at home), the financial aspect is important. How much money do you make when working, and what will child care cost? That said, when doing a cost-benefit analysis, non-financial benefits and costs should also be considered. For example, do you enjoy your job and are you excited to go back to work? Or will you love teaching and being with your child all day? You may also want to consider what type of experience you want your child to have. Daycare, home care, nanny care, or being cared for by a parent each have different costs and different experiences."

— Jennifer Jones, CPA, CA

PARENT'S TIP

"The best advice for new parents is to do a trial run and live on one salary for a year. Bank the other salary and build up an emergency fund. If you can't afford to do that now, adding a child won't make it any easier."

— Zachary, dad of four

FINANCIAL TIP

"An emergency fund is an important goal to have as a buffer for the unexpected. This was definitely important for us during our first pregnancy. I was about to begin a position in Stockholm at a professional services firm the week of September 15, 2008. And then on Monday, September 8, the financial crisis began to affect the world markets and major financial institutions. By the end of that week my position had been rescinded. Luckily, we had the financial resiliency to survive this unexpected event because my wife and I had built up a three-month emergency fund as part of our financial-planning goals. An emergency fund can really provide an added level of financial safety against an unexpected event."

— Garth Sheriff, CPA, CA, dad of two

Median Child Care Fees for Daycare Centres and Home-Based Care for All Age Groups and Cities

(From the 2018 report prepared by the Canadian Centre for Policy Alternatives)

CITY	PROVINCE	INFANT FEE (monthly)	TODDLER FEE (monthly)	PRESCHOOLER FEE (monthly)
Vancouver	BC	$1,400	$1,407	$1,000
Burnaby	BC	$1,260	$1,200	$900
Surrey	BC	$1,250	$1,250	$850
Richmond	BC	$1,335	$1,200	$975
Calgary	AB	$1,100	$1,030	$1,015
Edmonton	AB	$975	$875	$835
Saskatoon	SK	$900	$790	$730
Regina	SK	$845	$650	$597
Winnipeg	MB	$651	$451	$451
Windsor	ON	$998	$868	$781

CITY	PROVINCE	INFANT FEE (monthly)	TODDLER FEE (monthly)	PRESCHOOLER FEE (monthly)
London	ON	$1,229	$1,131	$1,044
Kitchener	ON	$1,495	$1,139	$1,044
Hamilton	ON	$1,237	$1,156	$977
Brampton	ON	$955	$1,222	$1,146
Mississauga	ON	$1,591	$1,269	$1,127
Vaughan	ON	$1,411	$1,204	$1,085
Toronto	ON	$1,685	$1,367	$1,150
Markham	ON	$1,370	$1,130	$1,078
Ottawa	ON	$955	$1,009	$1,007
Gatineau	QC	$190	$190	$190
Laval	QC	$190	$190	$190
Montreal	QC	$175	$175	$175
Longueuil	QC	$190	$190	$190
Quebec City	QC	$190	$190	$190
Saint John	NB	$868	$716	$694
Halifax	NS	$967	$845	$867
Charlottetown	PE	$738	$608	$586
St. John's	NL	$977	$726	$760

CHAPTER FIVE

Government Benefits for Parents

IF YOU'VE MANAGED to fill out the paperwork for your child's birth certificate and apply for your baby's social insurance number (while trying to function in a sleep-deprived new-parent fog) consider yourself ahead of the game.

The previous chapters gave you an idea of how much this baby is going to cost you, but there is some good news! There are various government benefits you are entitled to; you may need to apply for them, but most of them will be calculated based on your income tax return.

In this chapter, we provide the information you need to apply for those benefits.

Note: All benefit amounts quoted in this chapter were current as of 2019 and 2020 (where available), based on information provided on provincial and federal websites. To calculate your benefits, please see the Canada Revenue Agency's Child and Family Benefits Calculator (see Chapter 8).

Federal Government Benefits for Parents

A new baby not only means you have a dependent to claim at tax time, it also means you could qualify for a number of benefits from the federal and/or provincial governments to help you raise your new arrival.

Canada Child Benefit (CCB)

The CCB came into effect on July 1, 2016, and it is offered in all provinces and territories. (It replaced the former Canada Child Tax Benefit and the Universal Child Care Benefit.) When you register your child's birth with your province (you'll get the necessary paperwork from your health care provider), the information is shared with the CRA. From there, the CRA determines eligibility for the CCB and any related provincial programs (read on for these benefits). "In my experience, the process was quick and seamless and I received notification in a few weeks," says Pat Kenney, CPA, CA.

There are key differences between the CCB and the Universal Child Care Benefit — the latter was a taxable, fixed amount paid monthly to every family with children younger than seventeen, and it was paid regardless of a family's income. The CCB, on the other hand, is a nontaxable monthly payment based on a family's net income. Families will receive the maximum amount ($6,765 annually per child younger than six and up to $5,708 annually per child aged six to seventeen) if their net income is $31,000 or less. "As the family net income surpasses $30,000, the amount received is reduced by specific factors based on the total net income and the number of children," says Candice Hartwell, CPA, CMA.

What You Will Receive

Go to Canada.ca, click on the Taxes tab, and click on the Child and Family Benefits Calculator to find out what you're entitled to.

Eligibility

You must meet all of the following conditions:

- your child must live with you
- you must be primarily responsible for his or her care and upbringing

- you must be a resident of Canada
- you or your spouse or common-law partner must be a Canadian citizen, permanent resident, protected person, or temporary resident who has lived in Canada for the past eighteen months and has a valid permit

How to Apply

You can apply if you're the parent of a newborn living in any Canadian province or territory. Apply using the Automated Benefits Application in the birth registration package you're provided with (you'll most likely receive this information before you leave the hospital with your baby) or complete Form RC66.

For more information on how to apply, see www.canada.ca/en/services/taxes/child-and-family-benefits.html.

HOW THEY DO IT

Kory's daughter was fifteen months old when she found out she and her partner were expecting again. While she had some financial concerns, Kory says she feels better equipped to handle what life will be like when baby number two arrives because of her experience the first time around. "We had a better idea what we'd spend going into this one, and because our kids will be so close in age, we already have a lot of baby stuff from our first child," she says. "We also worked hard to get our savings up as high as we could in order to feel a bit more comfortable, though we know we'll have to dip into them with two kids at home. Honestly, our biggest issue is daycare and how we'll afford spots for two kids. Diapers for two is also daunting," she laughs. "We talk about it a lot. We both freak out sometimes and have to remind each other we'll be okay."

Another thing on Kory's mind was losing her salary. "I make more than my husband, so we're really going to take a hit when I take time off. I work contracts, so I'm planning on staying home for the first six months, then I'll take a two-month contract so my husband can take time with the kids, and then we'll switch and I'll be home. He gets topped off for six weeks, so we decided we might as well take advantage of that — it will help."

Continued on the next page

HOW THEY DO IT Cont.

They've also discussed how to cut their spending while Kory's on leave. "I'll try to ease up on our grocery bills, and we won't be eating out as often. The biggest thing is that we like to travel, so we'll be scaling back on that or finding other ways to save so we can still take some time away. And if there are things we need that can wait until I'm back at work, we'll hold off. We need a new car, but that's going to have to wait. It's hard to scale back, but it can be done."

FINANCIAL TIP

"A large part of planning for our new baby was putting together a family budget. We try to review our budget as often as possible and make adjustments as we track our actual income and expenses with a budgeting app. Budgeting has become even more important as I begin to transition back to work and we arrange for child care. As the CCB amount will change annually based on our family net income and growing family, we've taken a conservative approach to not account for it in our budget. This gives us the opportunity to use any amounts we receive as 'extra' funds that we can use to help contribute to our son's RESP when we receive them."

— Candice Hartwell, CPA, CA

Child Disability Benefit (CDB)

This tax-free benefit offers funds to families to help care for a child younger than eighteen who has severe and prolonged impairment in mental or physical functions. The CDB is paid monthly as a supplement to the Canada Child Benefit.

What You Will Receive

You will receive up to $2,886 per year for a child under the age of eighteen with a disability, or $240.50 per month, which is paid monthly with the CCB.

Eligibility

Not every child who has a disability is eligible for the CDB — it is strictly for children under eighteen who have a physical or mental impairment that has lasted (or is expected to last) for at least one year.

How to Apply

You need to complete Form T2201 (Disability Tax Credit Certificate), and the Canada Revenue Agency will let you know if your child is eligible.

Note: Your child's doctor or another qualified practitioner will need to certify this information.

For more information, please go to www.canada.ca/en/revenue-agency/services/child-family-benefits/child-disability-benefit.html.

Adoption Expenses

If you've adopted a child, you may be eligible to claim up to $16,255 of expenses related to the adoption per child on your income tax return. You can claim these incurred expenses in the tax year that includes the end of the adoption period for the child.

Eligible adoption expenses you can claim are:

- fees paid to an adoption agency licensed by a provincial or territorial government (an "adoption agency")
- court costs and legal and administrative expenses related to an adoption order for the child
- reasonable and necessary travel and living expenses of the child and the adoptive parents
- document translation fees
- mandatory fees paid to a foreign institution
- mandatory expenses paid for the child's immigration
- any other reasonable expenses related to the adoption required by a provincial or territorial government or an adoption agency licensed by a provincial or territorial government

See www.canada.ca/en/revenue-agency/services/tax/individuals/topics /about-your-tax-return/tax-return/completing-a-tax-return/deductions-credits-expenses/line-313-adoption-expenses.html.

Check the appendix on page 101 for specific benefits you can apply for and/or receive from your province or territory.

CHAPTER SIX

Starting a Registered Education Savings Plan (RESP)

SAVING FOR YOUR little one's future education will be one of the most expensive investments you make. So how much do you need for your child's post-secondary education?

The average undergraduate tuition fees for full-time students for the 2010/2011 school year were $5,146, according to Statistics Canada. In just six years (for the 2016/17 school year), the national average rose about 24 percent to $6,373. By the time children who were born in 2018 start university or college when they're, say, eighteen in 2036, it is projected that families will be paying up to $80,000 for four years for an undergraduate degree (depending on the province) — and that's if your child gets a place in a local school. (Researchers have factored in a yearly increase of 4 percent in their estimates.) Those who plan to go to an out-of-town school and want to live on campus may be looking at more than $150,000 for an undergraduate degree.

What Is an RESP?

You'll hear a lot about opening an RESP when you're expecting and when you have a newborn. This special savings plan facilitates saving for a child's education after high school. Anyone can open an RESP account for a child, including parents, guardians, grandparents, other relatives, or friends. RESPs allow earnings within the plan to grow on a tax-deferred basis.

What's more, RESPs provide one of the few genuine "free money" opportunities offered by the Canadian tax system. The Canada Education Savings Grant (CESG) program (which you'll read about in this chapter) matches up to 20 percent of your annual RESP contributions to an amount of $500 annually (if you're putting in $2,500), up to a lifetime total of $7,200 per child.

If you're a middle-income family, you might also be eligible for an additional 20 percent of the first $500 in RESP contributions. Low-income families have access to the Canada Learning Bond (CLB), which is also covered in this chapter. This is money that the government deposits into an RESP and doesn't require you to make any deposits of your own. The total amount the government deposits can be up to $2,000.

RESP Keywords to Know

- the **subscriber** (parents, grandparents, aunts, uncles, etc.) makes contributions to the RESP
- the **promoter** (bank, financial services company) pays the contributions and income earned (called educational assistance payments, or EAPs) on the contributions to the **beneficiary or beneficiaries** (student or students)
- when contributions are made, a **government grant** (the CESG, CLB or provincial education savings programs) may also be paid into the RESP
- the **promoter** makes sure all amounts are paid into the RESP and can later make payments to the **beneficiary** for post-secondary education use

First, you will need a social insurance number for your child to open his or her RESP. Apply for one when you apply for the birth certificate. Any contributions made to an RESP by a subscriber are made with after-tax dollars, meaning there is no special income deduction or tax credit granted to the person contributing, unlike a registered retirement savings plan (RRSP). "As funds in an RESP grow and earn income, the income growth (or accumulated income) is not taxed," Hartwell explains. "However, once funds are withdrawn from the RESP to pay for the child's education, the 'growth' amounts — that is, any amounts over and beyond what was contributed to the account, the accumulated income — are taxed, but taxed at the beneficiary's tax rate." The original contributions to the RESP are returned tax-free.

Setting up an RESP account is simple — virtually all major Canadian financial institutions offer RESP accounts. Besides managing the investment side of the account, financial professionals will handle all of the administrative work that goes along with grants and withdrawals (for a fee, of course), says Kenney.

Why Do You Need an RESP?

Thinking about your newborn baby's post-secondary education probably seems a bit strange at this point — especially if you're still waiting to meet your new arrival! But ask any parent and you'll quickly discover that it won't be long before a university or college education is part of your hopes and dreams for your newborn and you find yourself doing the math. These days, escalating tuition fees plus dorm fees or rent, food, books, and transportation equal a huge amount of money for the average family.

Based on the incredible cost of schooling, you might consider reinvesting any child tax benefits you receive or asking grandparents and other family to consider monetary gifts that can be put into an RESP instead of spending money on toys, toys, and more toys for birthdays and holidays. "We have been very fortunate to have had friends and family offer cash as gifts for our new son," Hartwell says. "Although it has been tempting to spend these gifts on diapers (and caffeine!), we've been diligent in putting the money toward an annual RESP contribution for him. We have tried to make the maximum contribution each year to not only benefit from the government's CESG but also benefit from the power of compound interest." If possible, suggests Hartwell, parents should try to contribute the maximum amount as early in the calendar year as possible (instead of the at end of the year) to benefit from an extra year's worth of interest-earning potential. "As we prepare for our son's first birthday, a number of our friends and family have asked us for gift ideas. We've suggested to them that the best gift of all would be the gift of education. With the gift of an RESP, not only would their gift grow by 20 percent (with the CESG), but their contribution could possibly double (or more) by the time our son uses their generous gift."

When Is the Best Time to Open an RESP?

The sooner you open an RESP for your newborn, the better equipped you'll be to help finance your child's post-secondary education.

Of course, as a parent-to-be or new parent, you have plenty of other expenses to consider before and after your little one arrives, and when you're moving from a dual-income household to one income being replaced by employment insurance, it can be daunting to decide whether you have even a small amount of available money to put into RESPs. "When to start contributing is a tough question to answer," says Andy Hammond, CPA, CA. "The best time to open one is as soon as you've applied for and have received your child's SIN. This will give you the longest possible time to contribute."

If, for example, you start an RESP as soon as you get your baby's SIN and can afford to put in $2,500 per year to reap the benefit of the government's maximum contribution of $500 each year, by the time your child is eighteen you will have saved as much as $54,000 (plus interest) for his or her education.

We know what you're thinking — your child will definitely go on to post-secondary school. But what if he or she decides not to pursue further studies? What happens to all that money you've potentially spent eighteen years socking away? The good news is that you won't be taxed on the amount you contributed to the RESP. That said (yes, there's a caveat), you will have to pay taxes on the money that you earned in your plan. "This money is called 'accumulated income.' It will be taxed at your regular income tax level, plus an additional 20 percent," Hartwell says. The funds you have put into the RESP are returned to you. The CESG, on the other hand, can be shared with a sibling if he or she has grant room available; otherwise, it must be returned to the government.

FINANCIAL TIP

"When deciding if you can afford to open an RESP, start by candidly looking at your budget. It's boring, but most people don't know what they're spending day to day. Knowing whether you have enough to contribute makes a difference."

— Andy Hammond, CPA, CA

FINANCIAL TIP

"Making regular payments instead of contributing a wad of cash in one sitting can take the sting out of putting money aside. It's easier for parents to set aside $20, $50, or $100 per pay than it is to put in a lump sum once a year."

— Julie Langevin, CPA, CA

FINANCIAL TIP

"It's important to start contributing to RESPs early in a child's life for two reasons. The first is simple enough — to build up a sizable investment portfolio to realize the magic of compounding interest. The second is because the government limits annual CESG payments to $1,000 when 'catch-up' contributions are made. For example, if an RESP is opened at age five and $7,500 is contributed, the 20 percent CESG match will only be calculated on $5,000. For those late to the game, the ideal strategy is therefore to contribute $1,000 each year until the CESG has been received for all missed years. To put numbers to this (and sticking with opening the RESP at age five), if $5,000 is contributed in years five, six, seven, and eight, the CESG will ultimately be recovered for years one to four. Be aware there is no proration of the CESG in the year of birth."

— Pat Kenney, CPA, CA

Registered Retirement Savings Plans (RRSPs), Tax-Free Savings Accounts (TFSAs), or RESPs?

Should you be putting money into RRSPs, TFSAs, or RESPs? In layman's terms, RRSPs are savings programs that incentivize individuals to save for the future by using tax deferral as the "carrot," explains Hartwell. The RRSP allows you to invest a certain amount each year (based on your prior year's net income) into a registered savings plan. When you do this, the government will reduce your net income by the amount invested, which then reduces your income taxes for the calendar year.

For a typical employee, your employer would have already remitted any income tax you would have owed throughout the year. By reducing your net income by the amount of your RRSP contribution, you are eligible to have the income taxes previously remitted to the government returned to you as a tax refund or as a reduction of any taxes owing on your tax return. Hartwell says a key strategy is to invest in an RRSP in the years when you are earning more (and are in a higher tax bracket) and to withdraw those funds in years when you are in a lower tax bracket (retirement or perhaps even during maternity leave, if you need it).

The TFSA is another tool that can help you save money — it is a vehicle that can grow your money tax-free throughout your lifetime. Contributions to a TFSA are not deductible for income-tax purposes. The income that's earned in the account (for example, investment income and capital gains) is tax-free, even when it's withdrawn. The nice thing about the TFSA is that it's flexible. It can act as a simple savings account that doubles as your emergency fund or an investment account.

Of course there are similarities between the TFSA and RRSP. Both have contribution limits, and in both cases contributions are cumulative, which means if you don't use them this year, they will be carried forward until you do. One of the main differences is that your RRSP contribution is tax-deductible and you'll eventually have to pay the tax you save from the contribution when you withdraw it in your retirement. (When you withdraw from your RRSP account, that amount becomes part of your yearly income and will be taxed at your current income-tax bracket.)

Your TFSA contributions are not tax-deductible, but any gains in the account can be withdrawn tax-free. (Any amount in that account is withdrawn tax-free, and in retirement you wouldn't have to worry about planning the timing of its withdrawal.)

As for RESPs and RRSPs, there are also commonalities. "For starters, on a contribution being made to either, an immediate tax perk is received. Beyond contribution and investment, another perk is that the funds in the accounts grow tax-free, which accelerates the magic of compound interest (income)," says Kenney. And here's another parallel — "eventually, the CRA does come knocking for their tax dollars. RRSP withdrawals are fully taxable to the contributor (ignoring certain income-splitting provisions) and RESP withdrawals are fully taxable but to the student recipient."

FINANCIAL TIP

"Consider a preauthorized automatic payment plan for your RESP contribution. We hear of these often for a reason — they are simple and they work. Having amounts coming right off your paycheque on payday into your RESPs is a great way to hit your financial goals. There is no shortage of demand to invest your hard-earned dollars, and accordingly all the financial institutions out there make it ultra-convenient to set up these plans."

— Pat Kenney, CPA, CA

FINANCIAL TIP

"You shouldn't worry if you can't afford to open an RESP and get the maximum government benefit. I've not met anyone who has been able to do this. We all want to do the best we can for our kids, but new parents feel a tremendous amount of pressure to open RESPs and contribute to RRSPs and to a TFSA, and they shouldn't. If you're getting by during this transition time, that's good enough. If you can't afford to contribute to an RESP, accept it and leave it at that. Most university and college students work to cover their tuition, and that will be a very good thing for little Johnny or Jane."

— Andy Hammond, CPA, CA

FINANCIAL TIP

"Thanks to the power of compound interest, once the money is set aside into an RESP, it starts earning income on its own."

— Julie Langevin, CPA, CA

When *Not* to Open an RESP

The experts are pretty much on the same page on this one — it's not the right time to contribute to RESPs if, quite simply, you don't have money left over each month after paying the mortgage, car payments, buying groceries, etc. Also, don't do it if it means going further into debt just to open this savings vehicle. "And absolutely don't contribute to one if you're carrying credit card balances — the high interest rates on those will kill you every time," Hammond says.

That said, even if you don't have funds to contribute to an RESP — and if your family earns less than $45,282 per year — some experts suggest opening one anyway, since the Government of Canada will deposit money to help you get started saving. The Canada Learning Bond (more on this later) provides up to $2,000 per child over fifteen years — $500 is received at birth and $100 is received each year that the child and family qualify.

If you haven't been setting money aside, don't worry about any years you've missed contributing — Julie Langevin, CPA, CA, says there are ways to catch up later if this is the situation you're currently in: "It's okay to contribute while paying off debt as long as families are actually paying off their debt and not adding to it. One way of doing this is by making regular payments every month. Set it up as automatic payments and see the debt balance go down and the RESP account go up."

RESPs and Taxation

First, RESPs are not taxed until the amount is withdrawn to cover education costs. It's important to remember that the income earned by investments gets taxed eventually — "there is no type of investment income out there where you don't get taxed. The big question is when the tax hits," says Adrian Dastur, CPA, CGA, CA. By contributing to RESPs, Dastur says you're simply delaying when the tax man comes knocking. "The interest that you earn in an RESP account is allowed to grow tax-free. Nobody pays tax on this interest while the money is earning interest in the cocoon of the RESP."

Fast-forward eighteen years and your child has grown up and is ready to pay for school. "The time has come to extract the money from the RESP, and you're removing money from that protective cocoon to give to the beneficiary," Dastur explains. "The interest income earned over the years will now get taxed in the hands of the person who received the money. The payments that the student receives out of the RESP will get treated as income. The nice thing is that most students don't have a lot of income to declare, so they are already at a lower tax bracket." Plus, don't forget the education credit from the government (the CESG) — this is an additional tax savings for the student, on top of the lower tax bracket.

You can also minimize tax on RESP withdrawals by estimating your student's other tax credits, deductions, and income sources, such as summer jobs and part-time work through the school year. The typical student's tax-efficient withdrawal is $11,636 plus tuition credits minus employment income. "For the hands-on student, plugging estimates into any of the popular tax-preparation software packages until tax payable is nil, or close to, is a great way to determine the sweet spot for withdrawals," Kenney says.

For more information on RESPs, see www.canada.ca/en/revenue-agency/services/tax/individuals/topics/registered-education-savings-plans-resps/special-rules/transferring-resp-property-another-resp.html. A financial professional will be able to give you advice on contributions tailored to your family's lifestyle and current financial situation.

FINANCIAL TIP
"I would absolutely recommend families use their Canada Child Benefit payments to contribute to a child's RESP. In some cases, a *Continued on the next page*

FINANCIAL TIP Cont.
family could contribute the maximum to a child's RESP and still come up short in funding 100 percent of post-secondary education costs. In addition to maxing out RESP contributions, savvy parents might also consider putting all or a portion of their child's CCB payments in an in-trust-for (ITF) investment account in their child's name. Other legitimate monies the child receives, such as birthday and other gifts, would do the trick here as well. The accumulated ITF savings can then be used to supplement RESP savings." — Pat Kenney, CPA, CA

FINANCIAL TIP
"It's a great idea to use the Canada Child Benefit to contribute to a child's registered education savings plan, if it's possible to do so. Families need to be aware of their outflows — they may not be able to tuck away the CCB if they need the funds. From a personal standpoint, I will say that we don't move the CCB payment we receive to an RESP because we have significant daycare costs. We have two kids and pay more than $2,100 a month on daycare because we don't have alternative child care options such as family to watch the kids. I am sure a lot of families who live in cities with a higher cost of lodging and living are also faced with this, and may not be able to afford to save the CCB payment." — Adrian Dastur, CPA, CGA, CA

The Flexibility of RESPs

"The RESP program includes considerable flexibility to accommodate the uncertainty of future academic pursuits," Kenney says. First, contributions can be made to age thirty-one, and accounts can remain open until age thirty-six. "The list of eligible institutions is vast and goes well beyond the 'name brand' universities and community colleges. Technical, vocational and trade schools generally qualify." You can find a full list of designated education institutions on the federal government's website. Keep in mind that RESP savings can also be used for costs beyond tuition, such as books, room and board, and living expenses.

There are three types of RESP plans: individual plans, family plans, and group plans. Individual plans have one named beneficiary and the person opening the plan does not have to be related to the beneficiary. Family plans can name more than one beneficiary, but the person opening the plan must be related to the beneficiaries. Finally, a group plan is for one beneficiary only and the beneficiary does not need to be related to the person opening the plan.

RESPs can (and most financial experts agree should) be set up as family plans, which pool funds and are divvied up amongst siblings according to needs. "With the cost of schooling on the rise, it wouldn't be unheard of for a family plan to be set up for, say, two children, and then one ends up deciding that post-secondary isn't for him or her. In this case, the entire account is consumed by the remaining scholar," explains Kenney. It's also important to note that if all children end up deciding to go on to post-secondary education, funds don't necessarily have to be divided equally. "This can be advantageous when, for example, one child decides to go to medical school and the other pursues less expensive and shorter term vocational training," Kenney says.

Group plans are provided by group plan dealers and each group plan is different and has its own rules. The savings are combined with those of other people and how much each child gets depends on how much money is in the group account, and the number of students of the same age who are in school that year.

There is a downside to group plans — some require minimum contributions every year, and if for unforeseen reasons you can't keep up, Kenney says you run the risk of losing your contributions to date (which accrue to the remaining plan members as a benefit). You generally have less control over what you're investing in with group plans, but the vast majority of us are happy to leave investing to professionals. "Many of us do just fine in family plans. The key is to do your research, make the best decision for you, and then monitor and change course if needed."

When Children Don't Use Their RESPs

Think about what's sitting inside this RESP account when your child reaches eighteen years old, says Dastur. The total pot of money is made up of the following distinct pieces: the contributions you (or other friends or family) made into the plan; the government grants (CESG) that the plan received during its lifetime; and the interest or income earned by the plan during its lifetime.

If your child decides not to go to a post-secondary educational institution, you could transfer the funds into another child's RESP (or, if you have a family plan, other children will automatically get to use the money that their sibling didn't use). Dastur says there are a few rules to keep in mind about this — the main one is that this transfer will only work if you're not exceeding the maximum limits for the other student. If you can't transfer the money, you'll need to consider the three distinct pieces that make up the pot.

First, the total contributions made into the plan will be refunded back to the person who originally contributed to the RESP. "There's no tax applied on this refund amount because the original money used was 'after-tax money' and has already been taxed once."

Second, the CESG and/or other government grants received will need to be given back to the government.

Lastly, the interest that was earned during the lifetime of the investment (which was allowed to grow tax-free) can be paid to the person who made the contributions. "But since the tax was deferred on this investment, the government will now tax this income, which is only fair because the investment sat all of those years and was allowed to grow tax-free," says Dastur. A good option is to transfer this money into an RRSP. The money will continue to grow on a tax-deferred basis until retirement, when the person starts to withdraw money out of the RRSP.

Canada Education Savings Grant

The federal government currently offers a matching grant incentive of 20 percent of annual contributions to an RESP, to a maximum amount of $500 annually (slightly higher for families with a modest income) and a lifetime total of $7,200 per child. It's available to all Canadians, regardless of your family's income. Families earning income less than

$45,917 will receive an additional 20 percent on the first $500 of RESP contributions ($100), and families earning between $45,917 and $91,832 receive an additional 10 percent on the first $500 of RESP contributions ($50). "I view the CESG as a guaranteed 20 percent rate of return, which is as good as it gets in today's marketplace," Kenney says.

This grant really helps parents save for their child's post-secondary education; the money is deposited directly into the child's RESP. There's an incentive for families to make the maximum contribution as early as possible in their child's life to reap the biggest financial rewards later. Ideally, a family would contribute the maximum $2,500 at the beginning of the calendar year, then save $208.33 each month ($2,500 over twelve months) to have enough room to contribute the next January.

Kenney says it's important to be mindful of the CESG hitting that ceiling of $7,200 per child. "Based on the $500 annual CESG maximum, families contributing $2,500 each year from birth will hit the $7,200 CESG ceiling around a child's fifteenth birthday and $36,000 in contributions. As the maximum lifetime contribution is $50,000 and contributions can be made until he or she turns thirty-one, this begs the question of what to do when the CESG is no longer on the table but saving dollars are available." Kenney advises turning focus first to other tax-preferred vehicles which are available to the family — RRSPs or a TFSA for parents, RESPs for other children, and registered disability savings plan for children (if applicable). Children will start to accumulate TFSA room when they turn eighteen and may have accumulated some RRSP room if they worked and filed taxes in their teens. "These are likely to be more advantageous than contributing to an RESP with no CESG up for grabs," adds Kenney.

The CESG is not taxable on receipt. Instead, it is taxed at the end when the student withdraws the accumulated amounts to cover his or her post-secondary education costs.

If the beneficiary does not continue his or her education past high school, the CESG is returned to the government, along with any interest that's been earned. This sounds a bit daunting, but the money should be safe in the account and left untouched, so there isn't anything to fret over when it's returned. As for the income that's earned on contributions (for both the CESG and the Canada Learning Bond, which we'll discuss next), up to $50,000 can be transferred to your RRSP, if you have contribution room available. (If you don't, you'll be taxed on the income at your marginal tax rate, plus 20 percent.) "Being hit up for an additional 20 percent tax will undoubtedly sting for a period of time," Kenney says. "That said, with all the flexibility and upside, putting an RESP in place at an early age is a no-brainer to me."

See www.canada.ca/en/revenue-agency/services/tax/individuals/topics /registered-education-savings-plans-resps/canada-education-savings-programs-cesp/canada-education-savings-grant-cesg.html for more details.

Canada Learning Bond

The CLB is money that the Government of Canada can deposit directly into RESPs of children from families with lower incomes (less than $45,282 per year). You don't have to put any money into an RESP to reap this benefit — you simply need to make an appointment with the bank or financial institution you used to open the RESP and they'll help you apply for the CLB. Then the government will add $500 to the RESP. Depending on your child's eligibility (your net income), the government will add $100 per year until his or her fifteenth birthday ($2,000 total).

Eligibility

The Canada Learning Bond is only available to children:

- who were born after December 31, 2003; and
- whose families receive the National Child Benefit Supplement

See www.canada.ca/en/employment-social-development/services/learn ing-bond.html for more information.

Provincial Education Savings Programs

British Columbia and Quebec each offer additional education savings grants. This means that if you live in one of these two provinces, you can save money faster!

British Columbia Training and Education Savings Grant (BCTESG)

Families in British Columbia are encouraged to start planning and saving early for their children's post-secondary education or training programs. To help, the BC government will contribute $1,200 to eligible children through the BCTESG.

Eligibility
To be eligible for the $1,200 BCTESG:

- you must have an RESP with a financial institution that offers the grant
- you and your child must be residents of BC
- your child must have been born in 2006 or later
- the application must be submitted any time between your child's sixth birthday and the day before his or her ninth birthday
- your child must be named as a beneficiary of an RESP

See www2.gov.bc.ca/gov/content/education-training/k-12/support/bc-training-and-education-savings-grant.

Quebec Education Savings Incentive (QESI)

This tax measure encourages families in Quebec to save early for their children's education by offering a refundable tax credit paid directly into an RESP that offers QESI. You must apply for it with Revenu Québec.

See www.revenuquebec.ca/en/citoyen/situation/placements/iqee/default.aspx.

CASE STUDY: Two Takes

Kim, a new mom living in Toronto with her partner, has been paying closer attention to their budget now that she's on maternity leave. She currently puts $200 into RRSPs each month, she holds a credit card balance, and she has a big mortgage that she freely admits will be tough to carry on one income. She's not sure whether she should continue contributing $200 to her RRSPs each month (a fairly substantial $2,400 for the year), or whether she should move those funds into RESPs, stop contributing altogether and put it on the credit cards, or keep that money to make their mortgage payments.

1. Candice Hartwell, CPA, CA: "It's hard enough to keep track of the day of the week during maternity leave, let alone your family's finances. I would recommend Kim pause her RRSP payments during her leave. As she will likely only be receiving employment insurance, her personal income will be lower this year, leaving little incentive to make an RRSP contribution and benefit from its tax deferral arrangement.

   "Now, there is a big benefit to contributing to an RESP. If Kim makes the maximum contribution this year ($2,500), her child will benefit not only from the government's $500 CESG contribution (a 20 percent boost), but also from any interest and/or earnings on her contribution over the long term.

   "However, with interest rates on credit cards nearing 20 percent, any balance owing on her personal credit card is an urgent concern, especially as any missed payments can significantly impact her credit rating and possibly affect her mortgage renewal application in the future. To be conservative, I'd recommend Kim focus on repaying her credit card debt first, then focus on making RESP contributions. Even if she's unable to make an RESP contribution this year, she can make a contribution next year and still benefit from the CESG from both the previous and current years."

2. Pat Kenney, CPA, CA: "As a new parent living through inter-rupted paycheques and an assortment of never-before-seen bills, I

certainly empathize with Kim and her partner's muddied financial situation.

"To start, if Kim has a sizable balance on her credit card, this is the logical place to start focusing her family savings. New parents or otherwise, paying off credit card debt is always a guaranteed double-digit rate of return (often more than 20 percent). This kind of return rarely exists in today's marketplace, and never risk free.

"The only time I might advocate carrying a credit card balance for a period of time is if the payments are getting in the way of servicing the mortgage. This would of course be a short-term approach to hang onto the home, to be discontinued on Kim's returning to work. If this is Kim's situation, it would be prudent to make the minimum payment in preserving her credit score.

"Moving past the debt, let's hope Kim and her partner have adjusted their spending appropriately and have something left over after servicing debt. If so, the RRSP is unlikely the best use of funds for Kim currently. (RRSPs work best for those in higher tax brackets — more 'bang for your buck.')

"As Kim isn't working, she is likely in a lower tax bracket. If they insist on a household RRSP contribution, her working partner should be the one to do it.

"If Kim's budget came down to contributing to just one of either an RESP or RRSP, I would lean toward the RESP. As we know, the Canada Education Savings Grant from the government starts at a 20 percent return and only goes up if families qualify for the supplemental benefits. Also, using the Canada Children's Benefit to fully fund or top up a child's RESP and/or in-trust-for savings account is a tax-efficient approach to post-secondary savings.

"Kim and her partner are also prime candidates for key insurance products. They check all of the boxes: young children, big mortgage, and a heavy reliance on one or more incomes. They should be looking at term life and disability policies to supplement what they may have at work.

"Given the new addition to the family, I have this advice for

Kim and her partner: make certain your wills and power-of-attorney decisions and documents are current and include a guardianship agreement. Similar to the insurance policies, the process will take an investment of time (and money) to do it right, but the peace of mind that comes with it makes it a no-brainer.

"Finally, managing your financial and related affairs independently and successfully takes a certain skillset and considerable time. As a result, most of us are better off working with a team of professionals to hit goals and put appropriate safeguards in place. Your accountant is uniquely positioned to 'quarterback' all the functional areas amongst professional advisers."

More RESP Tips

- For every $10 saved into an RESP, the Government of Canada contributes at least $2 to the RESP account. The CESG provides 20 percent on every dollar for the first $2,500 saved in a child's RESP each year.
- Grandparents and other family members can get in on the saving action. Sure, presents from toy stores are fun for kids, but contributing to an RESP makes an awesome gift — one that will certainly last longer and be more appreciated down the road.
- If there's an age or health concern that the subscriber (the person who opened the RESP) might die before the RESP is used, the money can lead to issues between other beneficiaries named in wills. Name the parent of the beneficiary (the child) as a successor, and state in your will that account number 1234 is for little Johnny or Jane's education. Better yet, grandparents can contribute to RESPs in the parents' names.

CHAPTER SEVEN

Baby Number Two (or Three, or Four ...)

It's a Big Decision

IF YOU GOOGLE "Can I afford another baby?" you will find millions of results, including an incredible number of blog posts and forum conversations among parents discussing the financial pros and cons of doing it all over again and having a second (or third, fourth, etc.) child.

Your finances may be one of the most important factors to think about when you're debating whether or not to give your child a sibling, along with your age (and your partner's), health, career plans, and readiness. Any one of these can make or break your decision. However, it's hard to dispute the fact that having another baby when your pockets have been emptied and your bank account nearly depleted after the arrival of baby number one may not make the best financial sense for your family.

HOW THEY DO IT
Sara and her partner, Ahmed, have three kids — a four-year-old, a two-year-old, and a five-month-old whom they got pregnant with sooner than they'd planned or expected. "We didn't really have time *Continued on the next page*

HOW THEY DO IT Cont.

to talk about our finances before we got pregnant with Masoud. We had a toddler and preschooler and we knew we wanted to have another child, but it happened way faster this time," Sara says.

When it came time to figure out daycare arrangements, the family's finances played the biggest part in their decision for Sara to leave her full-time job, take a part-time position, and spend most of the day at home with their kids. "I was a full-time dog groomer before, but the cost of daycare would've been too much for us if I went back to work. Part of me wanted to stay home, but we can't afford for me not to be working at all," she says. "I'd like to run a child care business, but I can't because of our condo rules, so I've taken a job driving a school bus. I make an income and still spend most of my time at home. This is what works for us right now."

Things to Consider

First things first — if you're considering another baby, you need to think about the following factors.

Maternity leave: Will you take a full year, eighteen months, or will you have to go back to work early because you can't afford a year at home on EI instead of working and collecting your salary? And if you're having kids close to one another, have you been back at work for enough time to qualify for another period of EI? (You must have accumulated approximately six hundred hours or fifteen forty-hour work weeks, of insurable employment before taking another leave.)

Space: Do you have enough of it? Are you able to sell your five-hundred-square-foot, one-bedroom condo and buy a bigger place to accommodate your growing brood?

Vehicle: You might also need a car that can properly fit two (or more) car seats, followed by booster seats — are you ready to buy a bigger car and probably spend more on car insurance?

Baby equipment/clothes: Unless there is a lot of time between your babies, you'll probably still have all the basics from your first little one. But if you have bins full of frilly pink baby clothing and lots of girly toys from your first baby and you find out you're expecting a boy, you might decide to buy new clothes and playthings. And don't forget — if you've decided to have your kids closer together, your firstborn could still be using his or her crib, stroller, car seat, etc., which means you'd have to borrow or shop for a second set of the equipment you need.

Education expenses: Not only will you have an extra mouth to feed, you'll have an extra child to put through school (and sign up for hockey, dance, piano and swimming lessons, camp, and other extra-curricular activities).

And then there's the big one …

Daycare: Depending on where you live, you will probably find it difficult enough to find and pay for one daycare spot, let alone two. (See Chapter 4 for the average cost of daycare across the country.) Yes, the price of child care does decrease as tots age, so it's likely you won't be spending the full amount for two at the same time (unless, of course, you have twins!). But that doesn't mean it's not going to cost you a lot each month. By the time you're on baby number three, you could find daycare so far out of your price range that it makes much more sense for one partner to leave their job to stay at home.

Will You Stay at Home or Go Back to Work?

This is another key factor you'll need to weigh when you decide to add to your family.

The decision is often easier to make the first time around because having one baby at home is generally less work, less hectic, and less expensive than having a toddler or preschooler *and* a newborn. Being a full-time child care provider isn't a simple day job, nor is it easy to have to make a decision when both your finances and emotions are involved.

While you're weighing your options, you have to look at whether or not you'll be able to live off one paycheque — if you're not going back to work, you'll have to say goodbye to not only your salary but also the EI you're receiving while on leave.

Study the Numbers

Remember that budget list back in Chapter 3? You'll need to fill that out again, making sure to include all of your housing, utilities, transportation, food, life and health insurance payments, debt repayment, and miscellaneous expenses. Also, you need to add any contributions to savings accounts, RRSPs, and RESPs. Now track your expenses for a couple of months to see where your finances stand.

When you have a good indication of how much you're spending each month, do the math and figure out what staying at home rather than going back to work will look like. You can get rid of the costs of commuting, including public transportation or parking and gas (or both), lunches out and coffee breaks, suitable office attire and dry cleaning, as well as the money you'll save by cooking dinner instead of picking up pizza on the way home from the office in rush-hour traffic.

You can also strike out child care costs, because if you're at home, you won't need to spend a ton on daycare or nannies for the kids. (Hiring a babysitter once in a while is much cheaper than other child care options.) That said, if you do decide to go back to work, child care expenses you incur (including caregivers, daycare nursery schools, daycare centres, and educational institutions, for the part of the fees that relate to child care services) are deductible on your income tax return. Don't forget to factor this important point into your decision.

Once you've figured out the numbers, you'll get a clearer picture of whether or not the one remaining income in the family exceeds or falls short of your expenses. If you want to stay home but the numbers don't fall in your favour, there's still a chance that you can make it work if you do more cutting from your budget — that is, if you're willing to forgo monthly manicures, ordering takeout most nights, and that bottle (or two) of Shiraz each week.

Alternative Work Arrangements

Ways to Save If You're Going Back

If you decide you want to (or have to) go back to work, it's a good idea to talk to your manager or human resources department about the possibility of alternative work arrangements. Many companies are now offering flexible hours and work arrangements to accommodate their employees' busy lives.

Flex Time

Flexible work hours or "flex time" isn't new in the business world, but this type of arrangement — and others like it, including telecommuting and job sharing — are some of the most sought-after benefits in today's workforce, thanks to the growing importance placed on employee work/life balance. It's so prevalent that the 2017 federal budget included a measure to allow federally regulated workers the right to request flexible work arrangements from their employers. (While it's not mandatory for employers to grant every demand, companies that don't honour an employee's request would need to formally justify their decision.)

Not only can flex time help new parents get the most from their careers and family, studies show that there are many benefits to employers who allow their staff to work outside of the traditional workday: Employees tend to be happier, more satisfied, and more productive, and there are lower rates of absenteeism and turnover. One recent study found that when it comes to perks at the office, employees place the highest value on health insurance, followed closely by flexible work hours, more paid vacation time, and work-from-home arrangements. Workplaces that offer these benefits are seen as promoters of good workplace culture, which ranks high when choosing whether or not to take a job or to return to work following parental leave.

If flex time is an option for your family (that is, if your partner's or child's daycare provider's hours work with the hours you're proposing), consider talking to your manager about working from 7:00 a.m. to 3:00 p.m. or 8:00 a.m. to 4:00 p.m., for example. You might also consider asking about switching to a condensed workweek (working four ten-hour days per week instead of the typical five eight-hour days — this arrangement can save you a day a week of child care costs).

Working Part-Time or Job Sharing

If you can find a way to condense your duties, you might be able to convince your boss to let you work part-time instead of full-time.

If management doesn't see this as a viable option, you could make a case for job sharing, in which two employees each work half the time and each receive half the salary of what would be one full-time position.

For this arrangement to be successful, you'll need a colleague who's not only interested in job sharing but is someone you can trust completely (i.e., someone who has the same work ethic as you), because you'll need to divide and coordinate your tasks and responsibilities, as well as keep each other apprised of what's going on.

Telecommuting

Telecommuting, or working from home, once or twice a week is also a great option that many businesses are starting to embrace because it focuses on work/life balance. Employers are finding they're benefiting from the increase in productivity of employees — who are already armed with laptops, smartphones, and Wi-Fi — who can move from location to location (from home to the office or to client meetings) with ease.

PARENT'S TIP

"We always knew we were going to have a second child, and we wanted the kids close together in age — we just had to figure out how we'd do it. We did think about the cost of having two kids, mostly in regards to daycare, sports, university savings, and vacations. We cut out a lot of stuff to try to save money before our second, Nicholas, arrived, mostly in groceries and gas — we tried not to drive on weekends, for example. I didn't buy any maternity clothes; instead I borrowed from my sister, and we put that money aside to save for diapers. My husband's family lives in Italy and wants us to visit; four plane tickets instead of three means we might only be able to go once every five years. We figure we can pay for

Continued on the next page

PARENT'S TIP Cont.

both the boys to play soccer or a sport that's not too pricey. If they're both into hockey, which is way more expensive, well, we might have a problem. We really lucked out in regards to daycare — I was able to go back to work after my leave because my mom was willing to watch the boys during the day, which obviously saved us a ton of money. I probably wouldn't have been able to go back if we didn't have my parents. The financial aspect of having kids is really not easy to figure out.

"I suspect it will be even more difficult if we decide to have a third child."

— Shayna, mom of two

CHAPTER EIGHT

Resources

Pregnancy Financial Checklist

- Complete the Budget Template linked on page 48 to review your finances (see Chapter 3)
- Ask friends where to get great deals on baby equipment (new or gently loved items) and join parent-to-parent buy-and-sell groups on Facebook and other social media sites to look for second-hand treasures (see Chapter 2)
- Register for things you need and/or want so that family and friends can purchase gifts for you and for baby showers (see Chapter 2)
- Get the items you still need that you didn't receive as gifts, including diapers; note: you won't be allowed to leave the hospital without a car seat (see Chapter 2)
- Visit with your manager or human resources/employer and review your company's maternity/parental leave policy (see Chapter 3)
- Start considering child care options; you might need to get on a waitlist(s) in popular centres (see Chapter 4)

Government Websites

Preparing Financially for a Baby

www.canada.ca/en/financial-consumer-agency/services/starting-family.html

Budget Calculators

www.canada.ca/en/financial-consumer-agency/services/starting-family/
    get-finances-order.html
www.babycenter.com/baby-cost-calculator

Having a Baby

www.servicecanada.gc.ca/eng/lifeevents/baby.shtml

Maternity/Parental Benefits

www.esdc.gc.ca/en/reports/ei/maternity_parental.page

Quebec Parental Insurance Plan

www.rqap.gouv.qc.ca/index_en.asp

Canada Child Benefit

https://www.canada.ca/en/revenue-agency/services/child-family-benefits.html

Child Disability Benefit

www.canada.ca/en/revenue-agency/services/child-family-benefits/child-
    disability-benefit.html

Adoption Expenses

www.canada.ca/en/revenue-agency/services/tax/individuals/topics/
    about-your-tax-return/tax-return/completing-a-tax-return/
    deductions-credits-expenses/line-313-adoption-expenses.html

Provincial and Territorial Benefits

www.canada.ca/en/revenue-agency/services/child-family-benefits/provin
cial-territorial-programs.html

Registered Education Savings Plan (RESP)

www.canada.ca/en/revenue-agency/services/tax/individuals/topics/
registered-education-savings-plans-resps.html
www.canada.ca/en/financial-consumer-agency/services/save-resp.html

Child and Family Benefit Calculator

www.canada.ca/en/revenue-agency/services/child-family-benefits/
canada-child-benefit-overview/canada-child-benefit-ccb-calculation-
sheet-july-2017-june-2018-payments-2016-tax-year.html

Publications

Fraser Institute: "The Cost of Raising Children"
www.fraserinstitute.org/studies/cost-of-raising-children

MoneySense **magazine:** "The real cost of raising kids"
www.moneysense.ca/magazine-archive/the-real-cost-of-raising-kids/

Canadian Centre for Policy Alternatives: "Developmental Milestones:
Childcare Fees in Canada's Big Cities 2018"
www.policyalternatives.ca/publications/reports/developmental-
milestones

Canadian Centre for Policy Alternatives: "A Growing Concern: 2016
Child Care Fees in Canada's Big Cities"
www.policyalternatives.ca/growing-concern

Statistics Canada: "Survey of Household Spending (SHS)" www23.
statcan.gc.ca/imdb/p2SV.pl?Function=getSurvey&SDDS=3508

Other Helpful Sites

Multiple Births Canada
multiplebirthscanada.org

Adoption Council of Canada
www.adoption.ca

Related Provincial and Territorial Tax Benefits for Families

You do not need to apply separately for provincial and territorial programs unless you live in Manitoba. Manitoba residents have to apply for benefits (see the information below).

The CRA uses your Canada Child Benefits Application, whichever way you applied, to determine if you are eligible for provincial or territorial benefits and credits. If you are, they will automatically calculate your payments based on information from your (and your spouse's or common-law partner's) income tax and benefit return.

Alberta

The following credits are fully funded by the province.

Alberta Child Benefit (ACB)

Funded by the provincial government, the Alberta Child Benefit (ACB) is a nontaxable quarterly payment to help families with low and moderate incomes with the cost of raising children. This credit is paid to families with working income who have children under eighteen years of age.

You will get maximum benefits if your family's net income is $26,769 or less. Benefits are lowered above this level and are phased out when your family's net income is $43,303.

How Much Will You Get?

For July 2019 to June 2020, you may be entitled to receive:

- $1,155 ($96.25 a month) for the first child, plus
- $577 ($48.08 a month) for the second child, plus
- $577 ($48.08 a month) for the third child, plus
- $577 ($48.08 a month) for the fourth child

Payments are made separately from other provincial and federal (Canada Child Benefit) payments in August, November, February, and May.

How to Apply

When you submit an application for the CCB, the CRA will be able to determine if you are eligible for the ACB and if you qualify for additional benefits such as the Alberta Family Employment Tax Credit (AFETC).

See www.alberta.ca/alberta-child-benefit.aspx#toc-3.

Alberta Family Employment Tax Credit (AFETC)

Funded by the provincial government, this nontaxable amount is paid to families who have kids younger than eighteen and a working income.

How Much Will You Get?

For July 2019 to June 2020, you may be entitled to receive a maximum of:

- $801 ($66.75 per month) for one child
- $1,530 ($127.50 per month) for two children
- $1,967 ($163.91 per month) for three children
- $2,113 ($176.08 per month) for four or more children

The credit is reduced by 4 percent of the amount of the adjusted family net income that is more than $43,303. Payments are made separately from the CCB payments in July 2019 and January 2020.

How to Apply

When you submit an application for the CCB, the CRA will be able to determine if you qualify for additional benefits such as the AFETC.

See www.canada.ca/en/revenue-agency/services/child-family-benefits/provincial-territorial-programs/province-alberta.html.

British Columbia

There are two benefits paid to eligible families with children that are fully funded by the Province of British Columbia.

BC Early Childhood Tax Benefit (BCECTB)

This benefit is a nontaxable amount paid monthly to qualifying families to help with the cost of raising children under the age of six. The amount is combined with the CCB into a single monthly payment. It is calculated based on the number of eligible children you have and your adjusted family net income. Effective October 2020, the BCECTB will be replaced with the BC Child Opportunity Benefit (BCCOB), which will provide an enhanced monthly benefit to parents of children under age eighteen.

How Much Will You Get?

Families with a net income of $100,000 per year or less will get $55 per month ($660 per year) for each eligible child. The BCECTB is reduced if the family's net income exceeds $100,000 and is zero once the family's net income exceeds $150,000.

Eligibility

You must meet the following requirements to be eligible:

- be a resident of BC (on the first and last days of the payment month)
- be a Canadian citizen
- have an eligible child
- have a family net income less than $150,000 per year

How to Apply

The CRA uses the information from your CCB registration to determine your eligibility for the BCECTB. (If your child is registered for the CCB or was registered for the CCTB before July 1, 2016, he or she is automatically registered for the BCECTB.) You don't need to apply separately for the BCECTB. If your child is not registered for the CCB, you need to apply for the CCB to determine eligibility for the BCECTB. If you're eligible, the amount of any payments will be calculated automatically based on information from the tax returns you (and your spouse or common-law partner) have filed.

BC Child Opportunity Benefit (BCCOB)

This tax-free monthly payment will be made to families with kids under age eighteen effective October 2020. The maximum benefit is:

- $1,600 for a family's first child
- $1,000 for a second child
- $800 for each subsequent child under the age of eighteen

If the family's net income is more than $25,000 but less than $80,000, the BCCOB is reduced by 4 percent of the portion of the family net income over $25,000.

The BCCOB for a family with a family net income between $25,000 and $80,000 is not less than:

- $700 for the first child
- $680 for the second child
- $660 for each subsequent child under the age of eighteen

For families with a family net income of $80,000 or more, the remaining BCCOB is reduced by 4 percent of the portion of family net income over $80,000 until it is reduced to zero.

BC Family Bonus (BCFB)

Specifically for low- and modest-income families, an additional nontaxable payment (based on your income and the number of children you have) will be combined into your CCB each month.

The BCFB provides nontaxable monthly payments to help low- and modest-income families with the cost of raising children under age eighteen.

Benefits are combined with the CCB and the BCECTB into a single monthly payment.

How to Apply

When you submit an application for the CCB, the CRA will be able to determine if you qualify for the additional BCFB benefits.

See www.canada.ca/en/revenue-agency/services/child-family-benefits/provincial-territorial-programs/province-british-columbia.html.

Manitoba

Manitoba Child Benefit (MCB)

The MCB provides financial assistance that helps ensure parents will not lose all support for their children when moving off welfare. It also provides parents with additional assistance to help with some of the costs of prescription eyeglasses for their children.

Low-income families may be eligible for up to $420 tax free each year for every child. For a single parent of three children working full- or part-time and earning $15,000 or less, this totals $1,260, with partial benefits for parents who earn $15,000 to $25,000.

Eligibility

You must meet the following requirements to be eligible:

- be a resident of Manitoba
- have dependent children under the age of eighteen who are in your care
- be in receipt of Canada Child Benefits for dependent children
- have family income below a specific level based on the previous year's income
- not be in receipt of Employment and Income Assistance unless you are only receiving the health benefits portion of EIA

How to Apply

To apply for the MCB, you can download a printable PDF version of the guidelines for completing the MCB application and then fill out and mail in the printable PDF version of the MCB application, or you can call 204-523-5230 or 1-800-563-8793.

See www.gov.mb.ca/fs/eia/mcb.html.

New Brunswick

You may be entitled to more than one benefit in New Brunswick: the New Brunswick Child Tax Benefit (NBCTB), the New Brunswick School Supplement (NBSS), and the New Brunswick Working Income Supplement. They are combined with the CCB into a single monthly payment.

New Brunswick Child Tax Benefit (NBCTB)

Paid monthly and available to families who qualify who have children younger than eighteen, this provincially funded benefit is combined with the CCB.

How Much Will You Get?

You could be entitled to $20.83 per month (or $250 each year) for each child. This amount is reduced if your family net income is more than $20,000.

How to Apply

When you submit an application for the CCB, the CRA will be able to determine if you qualify for the additional NBCTB.

New Brunswick School Supplement (NBSS)

You may also be entitled to the NBSS benefit, which is included in the NBCTB. It's paid once a year in July to help families with the cost of back-to-school supplies. Families with a net income of less than $20,000 will get $100 for each child born between January 1, 2000, and December 31, 2012.

New Brunswick Working Income Supplement (NBWIS)

The New Brunswick Working Income Supplement is an additional benefit paid to families that qualify who have earned income and have children under the age of eighteen years. Benefits are combined with the CCB into a single monthly payment.

How Much Will You Get?

You could be entitled to receive up to $250 annually for your family. It is phased in once family earned income is more than $3,750. The maximum benefit is reached when family earned income is $10,000. If your adjusted family net income is between $20,921 and $25,921, you may get part of the supplement.

How to Apply

When you submit an application for the CCB, the CRA will be able to determine if you qualify for the additional NBWIS.

See www.canada.ca/en/revenue-agency/services/child-family-benefits/provincial-territorial-programs/province-new-brunswick.html.

Newfoundland and Labrador

You may be entitled to more than one benefit in addition to the CCB.

Newfoundland and Labrador Child Benefit (NLCB) and Mother Baby Nutrition Supplement (MBNS)

The NLCB is a nontaxable benefit is funded by the provincial government and paid monthly with the CCB to help low-income families raising children younger than eighteen. The MBNS is an additional payment for families who qualify who have a baby younger than twelve months.

How Much Will You Get?

As of June 2019, you may receive:

- $33.75 per month for the first child
- $35.83 per month for the second child
- $38.50 per month for the third child
- $41.33 for each additional child

If your family income is more than $17,397, you may be eligible for a partial benefit. For the MBNS, you may receive $60 per month for each child younger than a year old, depending on your family net income.

How to Apply

When you submit an application for the CCB, the CRA will be able to determine if you qualify for the additional benefits.

Newfoundland and Labrador Income Supplement (NLIS)

The Newfoundland and Labrador Income Supplement is a tax-free payment made to low-income individuals and families, as well as people with disabilities, who may be impacted by additional provincial taxes. The amount is calculated based on your family situation and your adjusted family net income.

How Much Will You Get?

The maximum annual payment amount if you have children younger than nineteen is $200 per child.

How to Apply

The amount is combined with the quarterly federal GST/HST credit payments.

See www.canada.ca/en/revenue-agency/services/child-family-benefits/provincial-territorial-programs/province-newfoundland-labrador.html.

Northwest Territories

Northwest Territories Child Benefit (NWTCB)

This benefit is a nontaxable amount paid monthly to qualifying families with children under eighteen years of age.

How Much Will You Get?

As of July 2017, you may be entitled to receive the following monthly amounts:

Eligible children younger than six years old:

- $67.91 for one child
- $122.25 for two children
- $166.41 for three children
- $203.75 for four children, plus
- $30.58 for each additional child

Eligible children from six years old to seventeen years old:

- $54.33 for one child
- $97.83 for two children
- $133.08 for three children
- $163.00 for four children, plus
- $24.41 for each additional child

If your adjusted family net income is more than $30,000, you may qualify to receive part of the benefit. These amounts are combined with your CCB into a single monthly payment.

How to Apply

See www.canada.ca/en/revenue-agency/services/child-family-benefits/pro
vincial-territorial-programs/northwest-territories.html.

Nova Scotia

Nova Scotia Child Benefit (NSCB)

Combined with the CCB, this provincially funded nontaxable monthly
payment helps low- to modest-income families raise kids younger than
eighteen.

How Much Will You Get?

- $52.08 per month for the first child, plus
- $68.75 per month for the second child, plus
- $75 per month for each additional child

Families with net incomes between $18,000 and $26,000 may be
entitled to a partial benefit. This benefit is combined with the CCB into
a single monthly payment.

How to Apply

When you submit an application for the CCB, the CRA will be able to
determine if you qualify for the additional NSCB.

See www.canada.ca/en/revenue-agency/services/child-family-benefits/
provincial-territorial-programs/province-nova-scotia.html.

Nova Scotia Affordable Living Tax Credit (NSALTC)

This is a tax-free credit that's paid to make life more affordable for low-
and modest-income individuals and families. It offsets the increase in
HST and provides additional income for these families.

This benefit is combined with the quarterly payments of the federal
GST/HST credit.

See www.canada.ca/en/revenue-agency/services/child-family-benefits/
provincial-territorial-programs/province-nova-scotia.html.

Nunavut

Nunavut Child Benefit (NCB)

This benefit is a nontaxable amount paid monthly to qualifying families with children under eighteen years of age.

How Much Will You Get?

You may be entitled to receive up to $275 per year for the first child and $75 for the second child.

How to Apply

When you submit an application for the CCB, the CRA will be able to determine if you qualify for the additional NCB.

Territorial Workers' Supplement (TWS)

Families who have earned income of more than $3,750 and who have children under eighteen years of age may also get the Territorial Workers' Supplement.

How to Apply

When you submit an application for the CCB, the CRA will be able to determine if you qualify for the additional supplement.

See www.gov.nu.ca/family-services/programs-services/nunavut-child-benefit-nucb.

Ontario

Ontario Child Benefit (OCB)

This nontaxable benefit, funded by the Ontario government, is offered to help low- to moderate-income families raise their children.

How Much Will You Get?

As of July 2017, the program offers up to $119.50 per month for each child under eighteen years old if your family net income is $21,887 or less. You may be entitled to a partial benefit if your income is above this.

The benefit is combined with the CCB into a single monthly payment.

How to Apply
When you submit an application for the CCB, the CRA will be able to determine if you qualify for the OCB.

See www.canada.ca/en/revenue-agency/services/child-family-benefits/ provincial-territorial-programs/province-ontario.html.

Ontario Sales Tax Credit (OSTC)
This is a tax-free payment that's designed to offer relief to low- to moderate-income Ontario residents for the sales tax they pay.

How Much Will You Get?
For payments based on the 2019 income tax and benefit return (July 2020 to June 2021), the program provides a maximum annual credit of $313 for each child in a family. If you are a single parent, or are married or living in a common-law relationship, the credit will be reduced by 4 percent of your adjusted family net income over $30,143. These payments are issued as part of the OTB on the tenth of each month.

How to Apply
The CRA uses information from your income tax and benefit return to determine whether you are eligible. You will receive a notice if you are entitled to receive this credit.

See www.canada.ca/en/revenue-agency/services/child-family-benefits/ provincial-territorial-programs/province-ontario.html.

Prince Edward Island

Prince Edward Island Sales Tax Credit (PEISTC)
The Canada Revenue Agency administers the PEISTC on behalf of the Government of Prince Edward Island. The PEISTC is related to the goods and services tax/harmonized sales tax (GST/HST) credit. It is a tax-free amount paid to help offset the increase in the sales tax for households

with low and modest incomes. This amount is combined with the quarterly payments of the federal GST/HST credit.

How to Apply

When you submit an application for the CCB, the CRA will be able to determine if you qualify for the PEISTC.

See www.canada.ca/en/revenue-agency/services/tax/individuals/topics /about-your-tax-return/tax-return/completing-a-tax-return/provincial-territorial-tax-credits-individuals/prince-edward-island.html.

Quebec

Quebec Child Assistance Payments Program

This is related to the CCB but not administered by the CRA. You'll need to file an application directly with Retraite Québec.

How to Apply

If your child is born in Quebec, there is no need to apply.

You must file an application if:

- you are an immigrant or become a resident of Quebec
- your child arrives in or returns to Quebec
- you live in Quebec but your child was born outside Quebec
- you obtain custody of a child
- you obtain or retain custody of a child following the breakdown of your union and you were not previously receiving child assistance payments in your name
- you obtain shared custody of a child
- you adopt a child
- the province asks you to apply for child assistance

For more information, see www.rrq.gouv.qc.ca/en/enfants/naissance/Pages/naissance.aspx.

Saskatchewan

Saskatchewan Low-Income Tax Credit (SLITC)

This nontaxable amount is paid to residents of Saskatchewan (and funded by the provincial government) who have low and modest incomes. Payments are combined with the federal government's quarterly GST credits.

How Much Will You Get?

As of July 2017, the program offers:

- for individuals, $346 per year
- for a spouse or common-law partner, $346 per year, and
- $136 for each child (maximum of two)

There is a family maximum of $964 annually. This credit is reduced when the family net income is more than $32,643 (families who earn more than this but less than $67,697 may be entitled to part of the credit).

How to Apply

When you submit an application for the CCB, the CRA will be able to determine if you qualify for the SLITC.

See www.canada.ca/en/revenue-agency/services/child-family-benefits/ provincial-territorial-programs/province-saskatchewan.html.

Yukon

Yukon Child Benefit (YCB)

Paid monthly and combined with the CCB, this nontaxable payment (which is funded by the territory, as well as Aboriginal Affairs and Northern Development Canada on behalf of Status Indian children) is to help low- and modest-income families with the cost of raising their kids to age eighteen.

How Much Will You Get?

If your family net income is less than $35,000, you could receive $68.33 per child per month. (You may be eligible for a partial benefit if your net income is more than $35,000.)

How to Apply

When you submit an application for the CCB, the CRA will be able to determine if you qualify for the YCB.

See www.canada.ca/en/revenue-agency/services/child-family-benefits/provincial-territorial-programs/yukon.html.

Acknowledgements

I'd like to thank CPA Canada for entrusting me to take on this fascinating subject and write about two things I'm passionate about: parenting and money issues. A special thank you to:

- Cairine Wilson, former vice-president, corporate citizenship, for giving me the opportunity to explore the topic and write this book;
- Doretta Thompson, director, corporate citizenship, and Li Zhang, principal, corporate citizenship, for their support and enthusiasm in getting this book to press;
- Tamar Satov, former managing editor at *CPA Magazine*, a dear friend and colleague who recommended me for this very exciting project;
- Michael Dave Dizon, art director, for his vision, and Mark Hinkley, graphic designer, for making sure the design perfectly accompanied the words;
- Maggie Tyson, former manager of editorial development and editor extraordinaire, for taking such care with my words and for the immense passion and excitement she brought to the book;
- Vivian Leung, program director for tax education at CPA Canada, for her incredible support and for sharing her invaluable knowledge of all things tax; and

- Cathy Hutchinson, the best copy editor in the business, for lending her eagle eye and catching those typos that always seem to creep in.

I'd also like to thank the talented financial professionals who lent their expertise:

- Cynthia Kett, CPA, CA, CGA (Toronto, ON)
- Virginia Tang, CPA, CA (Toronto, ON)
- Debra King, CPA, CMA (Edmonton, AB)
- Han Shu, CPA, CA (Vancouver, BC)
- Garth Sheriff, CPA, CA (Toronto, ON)
- Julie Blais Comeau (chief etiquette officer at etiquettejulie.com, Ottawa, ON)
- Kurt Rosentreter, CPA, CA (Toronto, ON)
- Jennifer Jones, CPA, CA (Vancouver, BC)
- Pat Kenney, CPA, CA (Mississauga, ON)
- Candice Hartwell, CPA, CMA (Burnaby, BC)
- Andy Hammond, CPA, CA (Ajax, ON)
- Julie Langevin, CPA, CA (Timmins, ON)
- Adrian Dastur, CPA, CGA, CA (Vancouver, BC)
- Vanessa Underwood, CPA, CMA (Toronto, ON)
- Vivian Leung, CPA, CA (Toronto, ON)

And a huge thanks to my friends and family for their encouragement: my parents, Debbie and Alan Goldman, for their support and for always providing free child care; my in-laws for opening RESPs for my daughters; my husband, Peter, for his excitement and patience while I wrote; and my two girls, Addyson and Peyton, who are truly worth every penny we've spent as parents.

— *Lisa van de Geyn*

About the Authors

Lisa van de Geyn is an experienced, multi-award-winning journalist, magazine writer, and editor. She spends most of her time writing about women's issues, parenting, health, and money for some of the biggest magazines in Canada.

She graduated with a Bachelor of Journalism from Ryerson University in Toronto and has held positions at some of Canada's most celebrated magazines, including *Chatelaine* and *Today's Parent*. She's also served as a writer and/or contributing editor at several publications, including *Canadian Living*, *House & Home*, *Best Health*, *ParentsCanada*, *Style at Home*, and others.

Lisa is the mother of two school-aged daughters, Addyson and Peyton. She lives just outside of Toronto and enjoys reading and her Netflix subscription.

Vivian Leung, CPA, CA, is currently Senior Principal, Taxation at CPA Canada. Prior to this role, she was Program Director for Tax Education, where she was responsible for developing and implementing the strategic direction of CPA Canada income tax education, creating or redesigning tax courses and programs, and overseeing their delivery. Vivian also works to advance the tax aspects of CPA Canada's Lifelong

Learning initiative for our members. Vivian joined CPA Canada from Ernst & Young (E&Y), where she managed the editorial review and ensured the technical accuracy of income tax titles in CPA Canada's Tax Reference Series and contributed to other CPA Canada and E&Y publications.

We acknowledge the sacred land on which Cormorant Books operates. It has been a site of human activity for 15,000 years. This land is the territory of the Huron-Wendat and Petun First Nations, the Seneca, and most recently, the Mississaugas of the Credit River. The territory was the subject of the Dish With One Spoon Wampum Belt Covenant, an agreement between the Iroquois Confederacy and Confederacy of the Ojibway and allied nations to peaceably share and steward the resources around the Great Lakes. Today, the meeting place of Toronto is still home to many Indigenous people from across Turtle Island. We are grateful to have the opportunity to work in the community, on this territory.

We are also mindful of broken covenants and the need to strive to make right with all our relations.